FEO, FUERTE Y FORMAL

John Wayne
1907–1979

It was with those words that John Wayne wished to be remembered and so it is only fitting that this biography of The Duke, one of America's favorite actors, open with them.

The phrase translates as "He was ugly, was strong, and had dignity." Beauty is in the eyes of the beholder, but John Wayne's strength and dignity could not be missed — on the screen or in person.

This is the story of John Wayne's life. We have lost a man, but the legend and the spirit and the works of that man will never die.

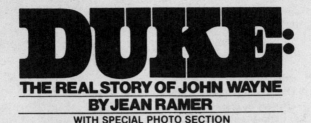

DUKE:
THE REAL STORY OF JOHN WAYNE
BY JEAN RAMER
WITH SPECIAL PHOTO SECTION

CHARTER
NEW YORK

AWARD BOOKS ARE PUBLISHED BY
UNIVERSAL-AWARD HOUSE, INC.
DISTRIBUTED BY ACE BOOKS
A DIVISION OF CHARTER COMMUNICATIONS INC.
A GROSSET & DUNLAP COMPANY

DUKE: THE REAL STORY OF JOHN WAYNE

Charter Books
A Division of Charter Communications Inc.
A Grosset & Dunlap Company
360 Park Avenue South
New York, New York 10010

EXCLUSIVE PHOTO ALBUM
CREDITS
Pages 5, 6, 7, 8, 10, 12, 13, 16, The Memory Shop
Pages 3, 4, 9, 14, Wide World Photos
Page 2, Republic

First Ace Printing, July 1979
Second Ace Printing, July 1979

2 4 6 8 0 9 7 5 3
Manufactured in the United States of America

CONTENTS

DUKE:
THE REAL STORY OF JOHN WAYNE

Chapter 1

GROWING UP IN IOWA

"My mother was always a little bundle of dynamic energy. Pretty, too—I think she looked a lot like Billie Burke. My height must have come from her side of the family, because her dad was six-feet-three. We couldn't figure out how she got to be so small and delicate-looking. She had a lot of strength, though, and she was a s spry and lively as ever, right into her seventies. . . ."

"My dad was a fine-looking man—a whole lot more handsome than I ever was. He was the kindest, most patient man I ever knew. People used to call him Doc because he had a way of handing out some helpful philosophy along with the prescriptions he filled at his drugstore. I don't

1

*think he ever made more than $100 a month. But
he gave me three rules that have guided me all my
life. . . ."*

It was spring 1907 in Winterset, Iowa, and Clyde
Morrison was getting ready to close up his drugstore for
the night. He looked over the record books he kept so
carefully. He hadn't done so badly.

The air, unusually balmy, wafted through the open
window and he breathed it in deeply. It was filled with
the promise of spring and summer ahead—the freshly
plowed earth, the fields of corn, growing from symmet-
rically planted seedlings into towering stalks, undulat-
ing in the breeze like a green sea.

Yes, Clyde reflected, Winterset was a good place to
be. Not much of a place yet—you probably couldn't
count more than 250 people in it, altogether—but it was
only about thirty miles from Des Moines, right in the
rich farm country, and bound to grow. And he owned
the only drugstore in it.

It was a good thing, because Molly was going to have
their first baby any day now. The time had gone so fast.
It seemed like yesterday when they'd taken their vows.

"I, Clyde Leonard Morrison, take thee, Mary Mar-
garet Brown. . . ." She was tiny, and red-headed,
and Irish, and pretty as a picture.

His thoughts were interrupted by the tinkling of the
front doorbell, followed by a quavery voice: "Doc?
Doc Morrison? You still here, Doc?"

"I'm back here," he called. He wasn't a doctor—

only a registered pharmacist—but the people had taken to calling him Doc.

The old lady shuffled up to the counter. "Doc, my arthritis is hurtin' me awful bad. Couldn't sleep a wink last night. Can you help me?" She showed him her gnarled, swollen hands.

"Well, let's see . . . ." He turned to his shelves and sighed. There wasn't much you could do for arthritis, he knew, except try to relieve the pain. He rummaged around until he found an ointment that would give at least temporary relief. He rubbed off the price with his thumbnail: $1.50.

"Now, you rub this in good tonight," he said. "It'll help you sleep. And go see the doctor."

"I can't afford those high-falutin' doctors," the old lady fumed. "Not on my pension!" She fumbled in her shabby coin purse. "How much do I owe you, Doc?"

"Fifty cents," he said.

"Ain't got but thirty-eight," she admitted. "But I'm expectin' another pension check any day."

He patted the gnarled hand. "Now, you just put that away. You can pay me when you can spare it. This winter's been hard on all of us. Thank the Lord, it's over. Pretty soon, you can sit outside in your rocking chair and let the good fresh air and sunshine work for you. That warm sun will do you a world of good."

"Thanks a lot, Doc," she mumbled. "I'll try that."

She shuffled toward the door, then turned and said, "God bless you, Doc."

With a tinkling of the doorbell, she was gone.

Clyde Morrison locked the door. He sighed again. The list of such "debts" on his books was mounting rapidly, and he knew practical-minded Molly wouldn't

3

approve. But you couldn't turn people away if they needed help that you could give them.

On the other hand, he wasn't doing too badly. Maybe he'd even be able to put in one of those new-fangled soda fountains soon.

On May 26, Molly began to feel the pains coming on and Clyde called the doctor. A while later—it seemed like eternity—the doctor arrived and went into the bedroom. It wasn't long before he emerged, grinning.

"Congratulations!" he announced. "It's a boy—and he's a husky young 'un. Haven't heard such a loud cry in ages!"

They named the baby Marion Michael Morrison. In those parts, where most of the people, like the Morrisons, were of Scotch-Irish-English descent, Marion was considered a highly respectable and even elegant name for a boy.

Certainly, a man as sensitive and kind as Clyde Morrison would never have given it to his first-born son in the same spirit as the man in the famous Johnny Cash song, who named his son Sue.

Nevertheless, the effect was pretty much the same. By the time he was old enough to talk and understand others, little Marion was busily bopping any little—or not-so-little—kid who taunted him about having "a girl's name."

In 1910, a baby brother was born. He was named Robert. At the time, his brother's arrival did not impress Marion one way or the other. The only thing that did impress him was being taken into the bedroom to see the baby and, after scuffling across the carpet, touching the metal bed with his foot and setting off a shower of sparks. He was sure he'd done something wonderful, like discovering electricity, until his dad explained that Ben Franklin had beat him to it by about 150 years.

When you're little you don't remember much, except for things like that, which for some reason are particularly outstanding. For little Marion, the most vivid and lasting impressions of his youth were:

Horses. He saw them for the first time in the barns of the local farmers. And what a thrill it was when they'd lift him onto the saddle and give him a ride! Then there was the added thrill of the great outdoors, the vast, breath-taking country of Iowa.

Football. From the time he was old enough to carry a ball, he loved the game. Sometimes the big kids would let him play because he was big for his age. He got roughed around a lot, but he'd always come back for more.

Fighting. If it wasn't about being named Marion, he was fighting in defense of his little brother, Bobby, who became his shadow as soon as he could walk. This resulted in embarrassing attacks, such as "Aw, why don't cha tell that little punk to go home?" To which there was no reply except, "He's not a punk! He's my brother, and he stays! Wanta make somethin' of it?" This was invariably followed by a flurry of small, flying fists, through which Marion, faster and stronger than most, usually emerged victorious.

The Three Rules. From the time he was old enough to understand, his father taught him three rules.

"They're the most important things you have to

5

know, son, all your life," his dad told him, sounding so solemn that Marion was terribly impressed. "Now, here they are, and don't you ever forget them:

"1. Always keep your word.

"2. Never insult anybody intentionally.

"3. Don't go looking for trouble—but if you get into it, be sure you win."

He was too little to realize the full significance of these three rules then, but he remembered them and tried to live up to them, always. The first two weren't so hard, but that third one was pretty tough!

His father's coughing. It started gradually, but it kept getting worse and worse. Finally, he'd come home from the drugstore too tired to play with Marion and Bobby, too tired to do anything but eat and go to bed.

Clyde Morrison had tried every pharmaceutical remedy he knew. Nothing worked. During the warm summer months, he'd feel better, and sometimes the cough would almost disappear. During those times he'd be hopeful that the cough was gone for good. But as soon as autumn came, with bone-chilling winds and rain, it would start again. As the cold, damp Iowa winter set in, the lingering cough became exhausting and almost unbearable.

"They didn't name this place Winterset for nothing," Clyde thought bitterly, as he dragged himself through the ice and slush to face another harrowing day in the drugstore after a sleepless night. It was hard on Molly and the boys, too, keeping them awake with his hacking.

Sadly, he looked around the drugstore with its neat,

well-stocked shelves. All his hopes and dreams for his family were in it. If he was seriously ill, what would happen?

Another attack of coughing hit him, so severe that he had to hold on to the counter for support. When it passed, he sank into the nearest chair, gasping for breath.

"I've been around sick people too long to go on kidding myself," he thought. "I just can't go on like this."

Going to see the family doctor was a last, forlorn hope. He knew what to expect before he got there, and the doctor, a trusted friend who'd cared for his boys since they were born, gave it to him straight.

"Clyde, you've got to get out of here," he said. "In this damp climate, that lung congestion of yours is only going to get worse, and what good is that going to be to your family? You need a hot, dry climate to get well—somewhere in the Southwest, maybe California. Another thing—I know how much that drugstore means to you, but if you could work outdoors, at least for a while, it would help."

That settled it. As soon as he could arrange it, Clyde Morrison sold his drugstore—for much less than it was worth—but it was enough to give him a start. He went to California by himself to look over the prospects.

Six months later he was back with great news—he'd bought eighty acres of farmland and had built a farmhouse.

The boys were overjoyed.

"Are we going to have horses?" Marion asked, eagerly.

"Guess so," Clyde said, smiling.

"Will there be cowboys and Indians?" Bobby asked.

"Well, I haven't seen any yet," Clyde said.

Molly wasn't so ecstatic. Clyde, a farmer? What did he know about farming? But she kept her thoughts to herself and started packing with her usual spunky energy.

With all their worldly goods, the Morrisons moved to California, none of them dreaming how deeply that move was going to affect all their lives—or that the little boy so inappropriately named Marion would grow up to be known throughout the world as John Wayne.

Chapter 2

DOWN ON THE CALIFORNIA FARM

"Our farm—if you could call it that—consisted of eighty acres in the middle of nowhere—a small township called Palmdale, right on the edge of the Mojave Desert, inhabited largely by rattlesnakes and jack rabbits. Those were the toughest times we had, but I learned a lot, too. . . ."

Palmdale, California, must have been named by someone who had a vivid imagination or was uncurably optimistic. In that dry, barren land on the edge of the desert, a palm tree didn't have a chance.

9

Molly's heart sank when she saw the farm Clyde had described so glowingly. It wasn't even cultivated. It was nothing but a big stretch of sagebrush and cactus. And the farmhouse he'd built could hardly be dignified by that name.

"Like it, Molly?" Clyde asked proudly.

"Well, it'll take some fixing," she said weakly. Then, with her usual vigor returning, she added briskly, "Now, just smell that good air. You're going to be better in no time!"

The boys were feeling let down, too. Peering as hard as they could, they couldn't see a single cowboy or Indian!

Suddenly, Marion shouted, "Look, Bob! Somethin's movin' over there!"

"It's just a jack rabbit, son," Clyde explained. "And you boys'll have to watch out for rattlesnakes— there's loads of them around, too. Got to get rid of all of them—they're just squatters on our land who'll ruin our crops."

In the days that followed, the one lucky break was hitting a very good supply of water, without the expense of having to drill deep. Also on the bright side was the remarkable effect of the hot, dry climate on Clyde's health. In a short time, his lung congestion cleared up and he felt stronger than he had in years.

It was a good thing, too, because getting the farm in shape for planting called for every ounce of strength he could muster.

Bobby was still too small to be of any help but, at seven, Marion was a big, husky lad. So from sunup to sundown, he was at his father's side, helping to clear the land and learning to handle a rifle. It wasn't long before his aim was as deadly as his dad's as the two of them blasted away at their enemies, the rattlers and the rabbits.

That was fun. But the biggest thrill of all was getting his very own horse!

Ever since he was a little boy in Iowa, riding was as natural to him as walking, but much more exciting.

His first steed was a brown mare named Jenny, and to say that she was a short walk away from the glue factory would be putting it mildly. In the eyes of her small "owner," however, she was the most beautiful, wonderful horse in the whole world.

Actually, Jenny served the practical purpose of carrying him back and forth to school, since the nearest school was eight miles away in the small town of Lancaster. In addition, Marion was charged with the important mission of going to the general store there to get whatever the family needed and bringing it home, strapped to his back along with his books.

Once, he got into trouble because a local busybody complained to the humane society about "that boy abusing that poor, old horse."

His teacher, who liked Marion anyway because he was a well-behaved boy and a good student, promptly went to bat for him in a defense he would never forget. "Nonsense!" she fumed to the authorities. "I never saw a horse better cared for in my life. Every chance he gets, he's out there feeding and watering her, and taking care of her. Man O'War couldn't have it so good!"

That settled it. He was able to go on riding Jenny to school—and to continue playing his favorite game. That was the best part of all.

On the road home, there was a huge cliff that jutted out so that you couldn't see the road beyond it. Well, maybe it wasn't so huge, but to him it looked that way.

"Careful now, Jenny," he'd whisper. "They're waitin' for us on the other side."

As they got close, he'd shout, "C'mon, Jenny, let's get 'em!"

Then, with great whooping and yelling, he rounded the cliff to face a "life-and-death" fight with the blood-thirsty band of desperadoes who were waiting to capture the treasure he carried on his back.

He was outnumbered! Bang! Bang! He picked them off with his trusty rifle! They got him! Mortally wounded, he gasped, "C'mon, Jenny, we've got to run for it!" And he'd urge her to the nearest excuse for a gallop she could manage to emerge triumphant with his "treasure"—probably a sack of flour.

There never was anybody there. There never was any living thing, except maybe a lazy old rattlesnake. But when you're a little boy with a big imagination, it could all be quite wonderful. It became a game he never tired of.

Jenny did get tired, though. One day, she just couldn't get up. She wasn't even interested in the food and water he'd brought her.

"Dad! Dad!" he shouted. "Something awful's happened to Jenny!"

Clyde Morrison took one look at the horse and knew how bad it was. He also knew he could ill afford a vet. Yet, seeing the hurt and fear in his son's eyes, he put an arm around his shoulders and said quietly, "We'll get the vet, son."

The vet came.

How do you tell a little boy that he has to lose the thing he loves most in the world? Between them, Clyde and the vet broke the news as gently as they could. It would be cruel, they explained, to let Jenny suffer any longer, when she was going to die.

In a way, the rifle shot that ended her life mercifully never ended her memory in the heart of her small owner. Her memory lived on, and all his life Marion would have a great kindness and compassion for horses. Anyone who mistreated them had to reckon with him—usually by getting thoroughy trounced— ''so you'll know how it feels, you rotten, lousy bastard!''

Life on the farm wasn't so good for young Marion after that.

Having to ride to school on a neighbor's buckboard wasn't much fun. But it wasn't just that change. He was old enough to realize that at home, things weren't going well.

Their meals had become scanty, to a point where they consisted mainly of potatoes or beans, presented in as many different ways as his mother could think of. Meat was a very rare treat. Lots of times, Marion and Bobby went to bed feeling hungry.

Tossing in bed, he'd hear his parents arguing through the thin walls. It made him feel uneasy.

''You have to face it, Clyde,'' his mother would say. ''You just weren't cut out to be a farmer!''

''But Molly,'' he'd protest, ''it takes time to get a farm going. You'll just have to be patient.''

"Patient!" she'd snap. "I've been patient long enough! How can we go on like this, with hardly any food in the house and the boys needing clothes?"

It went on, with the arguments getting louder and more bitter. It made him feel kind of scared. What if they busted up? Who'd take care of him and Bobby?

The last of a long line of crop failures settled it. With the best will in the world, Clyde couldn't hold on to the farm. He got what he could out of it, swallowed his pride and went to work as a pharmacist in somebody else's drugstore in Glendale, California.

Chapter 3

GLENDALE—A NEW NAME, A NEW LIFE

"There've been a lot of stories about how I got to be called Duke. One was that I played the part of a duke in a school play—which I never did. Sometimes, they even said I was descended from royalty! It was all a lot of rubbish. Hell, the truth is that I was named after a dog!"

In 1917, Glendale, California, was a thriving community, but still had a pleasant suburban quality. The Morrisons had no trouble in finding a nice little frame house on tree-lined Louise Street, not far from the drugstore where Clyde worked.

His pay was good for those days—thirty dollars a week. Still, there was only enough for the bare necessities as he was determined to have his own store again, and he put aside as much as he could manage.

For the boys life in Glendale was a whole lot better than on the farm. In fact, it was turning out to be quite thrilling!

The neighborhood kids soon introduced Marion and Bobby to what was to become their favorite hangout— the back fence of Triangle Studios, a few blocks away, where they were making "movin' pitchers"!

Every day, the cowboys chased the Indians and the cops chased the villains, through one two-reeler after another, and nobody seemed to mind the noisy back-fence audience. The actors weren't temperamental, and movies didn't have sound yet.

"Boo-o-o-o-o! S-s-s-s!" the kids chorused, when the bad guys appeared.

"Yay-y-y!" they yelled at the top of their lungs, when the good guys gave the bad guys their just deserts.

None of them loved it more than Marion, who yelled as loud as the rest. Soon he became ringleader in a new game they invented. A cigar box with holes punched in it became their "camera," and they used to shoot all kinds of "dramas," the more rough-and-tumble the better.

Just when cowboys-and-Indians was beginning to pall (to their mothers' delight), the game got a wonderful shot in the arm.

Clyde Morrison had finally acquired his own

drugstore and became friendly with another occupant in the building—the owner of a movie theater.

"Tell your boys they can come any time they want," the man said. "I'll let them in free!"

Sitting in the dark movie theater, watching the thrilling action on the screen for the first time in his life, Marion was fascinated. Soon he was going to the movies four or five times a week, and when *Four Horsemen of the Apocalypse* played, he saw it twice a day for a whole week!

Naturally, the cowboy stars were big attractions. Tom Mix, William S. Hart, Dustin Farnum, Hoot Gibson, Harry Carey—Marion liked them all, but he especially liked Harry Carey because he seemed so real.

His greatest favorite was Douglas Fairbanks. Ah, how strong and fearless he was in those duels to the death, how daring as he leaped from balconies and swung on chandeliers, how irresistible when he wooed the lady of his choice with that flashing smile!

Of course, all this information was brought back to his gang in order to make their movie-making game more exciting. And of course, Marion had to play all of Douglas Fairbanks' roles.

Jumping off walls and swinging on trees got to be too tame.

"Look out! Here I come!" he shouted one day as the "camera" was shooting "Doug Fairbanks" in his latest adventure.

Before anybody could stop him, he jumped out of a second-story window!

On the way down, he grabbed at some vines, in true Fairbanks style. But instead of swinging to safety as in

17

the movies, he brought a whole grape arbor down with him. It broke his fall and he wasn't hurt. Unfortunately, the grape arbor was—and so were its owner's feelings. That ended the game, for a while.

Besides a taste for movies, Marion also acquired a dog. It was a very large dog, of very doubtful ancestry, but that didn't matter to his proud owner. He named him Duke.

Somewhere in Duke's strange background there must have been a Dalmatian because he had a peculiar love of firehouses. Whenever he was missing, Marion would go the rounds of the engine companies, calling, "Duke, Duke! Here, Duke!"

The firemen got such a kick out of the boy and his dog that they took to calling them "Big Duke" and "Little Duke."

Though the fact that the name "Big Duke" referred to the dog instead of to him was somewhat painful, "Little Duke" liked his new monicker. After all, it was a whole lot better than Marion.

Somehow (probably with his own encouragement), the name caught on. By the time he was eleven nobody, including his own family, ever called him anything else. (In fact, they'd better not, unless they were looking for a fight.)

Through all Duke's Glendale adventures, Bobby tagged along happily. By that time, the newly named Duke realized that a little brother is as hard to get rid of as the hives, but he made the best of it.

When Duke was invited to a party, Bobby was automatically invited, too. This was fine, until a little girl Duke's age had a birthday party. After the cake and ice cream, the kissing games started, and one of the boys decided Bobby was too young for such grown-up amusements.

"Get that little squirt out of here!" he demanded.

"Oh, yeah?" Duke retorted. "He's my brother and he stays, see?" He accompanied his words with a swift punch in the nose.

At the urgent request of the girl's mother, the Morrison boys were forced to leave the party.

Duke was not to be defeated so easily. He rushed home, grabbed his trusty BB gun and, from a nearby hill, broke all the balloons strung up in the patio for the party, one by one!

Years later, he remembered the incident fondly, chortling, "I got every goddamn balloon! And you know, it was the only time in my life I really tried to right a wrong with a rifle!"

Life in Glendale wasn't all fun for young Duke. By the time he was eleven, he knew that if he wanted any spending money or new clothes, he'd have to get them himself.

He saw an ad for newsboys in the *Los Angeles Examiner* and applied. He got a job. When it called for getting up at 4:00 A.M. every morning to deliver papers, including Saturdays and Sundays, there weren't many applicants. To him the pay was worth it—a great, big six dollars a week!

Along with this grind, he managed to keep up with his studies. And a great honor, as well as his first public appearance, occurred at the graduation exercises at his grade school.

They'd had a competition for the best composition on any subject, and the winner was to recite it at the exercises. In what was undoubtedly a portent of the

man he was to become, he chose a political subject—
the wrongdoings of the Germans that led to World War
I. He won the competition.

Unfortunately, he had to recite the whole thing from
memory. That was all right, except he kept saying,
"And the worst thing the Germans done . . ." and the
teacher kept correcting, "And the worst thing the Germans *had* done . . ."

On the great night, he was going along fine, until he
got to that line. "And the worst thing the Germans *had*
done . . ." he proclaimed—and then his mind went
blank. He'd been so intent on getting it right that he
forgot all the rest.

Somehow, he managed to bow and get off the stage.
And to this day, he couldn't tell you what it was the
Germans *had* done!

Chapter 4

SOME HARD BLOWS AND A STRANGE FATE

"Ever since we moved to California, I loved the sea. More than anything else, I wanted to go to Annapolis and become an officer in the Navy. It was a terrible disappointment when I didn't make it. In a way, I guess I never really got over it . . ."

———————◆•◆▶◀◆•◆———————

A lot of things mold a boy into a man besides getting his first long pants and shaving and realizing that girls, hitherto regarded as abhorred creatures, are really pretty nice.

To Duke Morrison, two very important things happened in the fall of 1921, when he was fourteen: He entered Glendale Union High School, and his parents separated.

As devastating as this combination of events can be in a boy's life—as they must surely have seemed to Duke at the time—in a curious way they turned out to be beneficial.

Since he was eleven, he'd been on his own as far as earning money for clothes and spending was concerned. And he'd done his full share of work, running errands and delivering prescriptions and working as a soda jerk for his father. Now it was different. Suddenly, he felt a new, grown-up responsibility to his mother and younger brother.

If anything, the separation of his parents, much as he loved them both, was something of a relief. Young as he was, Duke realized that ever since the hard days on the farm his parents were poles apart temperamentally. His mother was peppery, practical and hard-working. His father was hard-working, too, but was a dreamer and philosopher whose schemes, somehow, just never worked out.

When it came, the separation was an amicable one, without destructive, bitter exchanges. It was agreed that the boys would live with their mother. But they could (and did) see their father often.

Spurred on by his new responsibilities as the "man of the family," Duke went to work with a will. During the summers and after school he worked at whatever odd job he could get—washing windows, picking apricots, driving a truck, mowing lawns, jerking sodas—anything.

Through it all, his record at Glendale Union High School was brilliant:

He played guard on the all-state football team.

He was president of the school's Letterman's Club.

He was head of the Latin Society!

He was president of the senior class.

He was a member of the debating team.

He was an A student, with a 96 average!

By that time in his life, he had learned that whatever he accomplished depended on his own efforts, and if he had to work harder than other boys, it didn't matter.

Sure, he'd have liked to go on lots of dates with the pretty girls in his class, but he seldom had the time or the money. He never became involved in a big high school romance, maybe because love didn't hit him, but more likely because he had other things on his mind.

Ever since he'd come to California and got his first glimpse of the vast wonders of the Pacific, he had one secret ambition—to join the Navy. He wanted to go to Annapolis and become an officer, in command of a vessel sailing those glorious, untamed seas.

In the back of his mind, this was another motive that inspired his great high school record. He knew that if he worked hard enough on his studies and on the football field he'd have a chance.

He got that chance. In the examinations for entry into the U.S. Naval Academy, he came in third in a group of thirty.

At the time, his rating was a very bitter disappointment. One that he never quite got over.

Still, he did have another opportunity. In his senior year at high school, his team won the Southern California Scholastic Football Championship. As a result, he was offered an athletic scholarship at the University of Southern California.

He decided to settle for that and study law. In fact, as he saw it, he didn't have much choice. It wasn't that law was especially appealing to him, but it was a good, solid profession, something to fall back on. With his father's business ventures consistently going awry, it seemed like a good idea.

The scholarship covered tuition only. Once more, Duke had to hustle for living money. He washed dishes in a frat house for his meals.

The first summer, he got a job with the Bell Telephone Company, for sixty cents an hour, plotting maps. As the second summer approached, they told him they didn't have any more maps to plot.

As badly as his dad's business ventures were going—his first drugstore had failed, an ice cream manufacturing company failed, and also another drugstore—he always sent his son five dollars a week. Duke, knowing what a great football fan his father was and how much he wanted to go to the games, saved the money and sent his dad a ticket for every game during the season. He told him he got them free. Actually, they cost him twenty dollars each. On the black market they were worth much more.

Unknown to Duke, another avid fan attending those games was one of his boyhood idols, Tom Mix. By this time Mix was a 20th Century-Fox superstar earning $17,500 a week. In another strange quirk of fate, these facts were to change Duke's entire life.

One day, on the practice field, Coach Howard Jones called him aside. "I hear you're looking for a summer job, Duke."

Duke told him he was and that his prospects were not only poor, but nonexistent.

"Well, I've got an idea," Jones went on. "Last season I got Tom Mix a good box, and he said if there was anything he could do for me he'd be glad to. So I want you and Don Williams to go over there to Fox. I'm sure he'll get you jobs."

The next morning the two boys went to the studio. To their surprise they were promptly ushered in to the presence of the great Tom Mix. More than a little awestruck, they stood tongue-tied while Mix strode up and down and, in the manner of a royal monarch being magnanimous to the peasants, proclaimed:

"Men, as a star I owe it to my public to keep in top physical condition. You are to become my trainers to help me do this. It will also be of benefit to you, because it will help you to keep in top condition for your sport, which I understand is football."

Duke and Don barely managed to mumble "Thank you, sir," before they were abruptly dismissed, with the directive, "Report to me personally when school is over."

Outside the studio, Don asked, "What'd you think, Duke?"

Duke shook his head. "Seemed a little balmy to me. But cripes, Don, I can't afford to pass anything up. Since that job with the phone company fell through, I haven't found a thing."

The first day after school closed, Duke reported to the Fox gate. As he stood waiting for the guard to check him in, a limousine that looked half a block long drove up. In the back seat was Tom Mix.

"H-hello, Mr. Mix," Duke ventured.

Mix looked at him vaguely—and drove on. "Well, that's the end of that job," Duke thought.

Just as he was about to leave, the guard called out to him. "You Morrison?"

"Yes."

"Go on in and report to the swing gang. Ask anybody. They'll tell you where it is."

"Well," Duke figured, "it's probably all some crazy mistake. But what the hell—I've got nothing to lose."

He found the "swing gang," and to his complete amazement, the boss, George Marshall, told him that he was hired at the magnificent salary of thirty-five dollars a week!

Duke never saw Tom Mix again. Obviously, he had kept his word to Coach Jones, and the star who felt he "owed so much to his public" gave them much more than he could ever have imagined.

A "swing gang," Duke soon learned, was just that. It swung into action—hard, physical work—doing all the menial tasks required in setting up, tearing down and keeping the action going on a movie set. It is an adjunct of the "prop" (short for property) department. Its principal function is to get the right stuff—whatever it may be—onto the set as fast as possible, remove it after the shooting and return it to the prop department.

As Duke toted loads of heavy equipment, he could see why this *was* a job that would keep a football player in training. He also learned an important lesson—that all movie-making is based on a time schedule that is invariably tight, demanding and essential to the financial success of the movie.

Chapter 5

FROM FOOTBALL HERO TO—ACTOR??

"When they tried giving me dramatic lessons, the teacher told me, 'Young man, you'll never be an actor in one hundred years!' I agreed with him, wholeheartedly!"

———————◆◆◆———————

"Hey, you! Get those goddamn geese off this set!"

These deathless words launched the movie career of John Wayne. They also marked the beginning of what he has often described as "the most profound relationship of my life."

As part of his job, Duke had been ordered to deliver some geese to one of the sets. He got them there, turned them loose, and all hell broke loose.

The geese were supposed to waddle around in the background, providing local color. They must have eaten some ham along with their corn because they refused to stay in the background. Instead, they strutted right up in front of the cameras, cackling like mad.

Duke stood on the sidelines, feeling completely helpless.

Pointing a finger at him, and fixing upon him the icy stare that was known to make important stars tremble, director John Ford told Duke what he could do with his geese.

"Yes, sir," Duke mumbled. Off he went, desperately lunging for the geese and tackling in his best football style.

The geese weren't about to give up their moment of glory. They dodged, they ran, they fluttered just out of reach.

Sitting in his director's chair, still trying to look angry, John Ford could hardly keep from laughing.

"That big, clumsy galoot!" he thought. But there was something about that boy. He seemed to be trying so hard.

Duke kept right on trying, but his next encounter with John Ford was equally disastrous.

One of his chores was to sweep up the cornflake snow as soon as a scene was finished, so that the set would be clean and ready for the next shooting.

One day, broom in hand, he rushed onto the set of one of Ford's pictures. As he started to sweep, an eerie feeling came over him. He looked up from his work.

There was the heroine, trudging tearfully through the snow in a poignant scene. And there he was, right behind her, standing with his broom.

"Cut!" Ford called wearily. That was all. And that was all as far as his job was concerned, Duke was sure. He had committed the unforgivable sin of blundering onto a set while the cameras were rolling.

But nothing happened. Ford, secretly amused, asked, "Who *is* that clumsy kid?"

In addition to these woes, Duke was getting the business from his fellow members of the swing gang.

"Hey, you're the guy who plays guard for USC, right?" one asked innocently one day. "Hey—show me how you get in position to make those tackles, huh?"

Obligingly, Duke squatted down. Whereupon one of the others gave him a swift kick in the rear that sent him sprawling in the mud.

Duke got up, burning from the humiliation and derisive laughter, and noticed that among those laughing was he nemesis, John Ford.

Quickly sizing up the situation, Ford walked up to him and said, "So you're a football player, eh? I'll bet you can't take me!" And he turned and ran down the field.

Still incensed, Duke went after him. With a few long strides, he closed the ground between them. A deft trip with his leg, a hit on the chest, and Ford went sprawling as ignominiously as Duke had a few minutes before.

His anger spent, Duke realized what had happened.

"Now I've really done it!" he thought. "I've roughed up a director!"

Ford got up, unhurt, brushed himself off—and burst out laughing!

He turned to Duke and held out his hand.

Duke returned to USC in the fall of 1926 with a happy heart. For the first time, he had money in the bank, the coming football season looked promising and he was assured that he would have his job in the prop department the following summer.

Because his finances had improved, he was able to go out on dates more often. So when one of his frat brothers came up with the proposition of a blind date with a beautiful señorita, Carmen Saenz, he took him up on it.

As a result, he fell deeply, madly, completely and irrevocably in love—with Carmen's younger sister, Josephine, who was dating someone else.

Wooing and winning the highborn, socially prominent daughter of the Panamanian envoy to the Consulate of Los Angeles (which is what Josie turned out to be), he knew wouldn't be an easy proposition for a college boy with only a scholarship and a summer job between him and starvation.

On the football field, he played harder and better than ever. That athletic scholarship just *had* to get him his law degree.

He played much too hard and suffered torn ligaments in his shoulder and an ankle injury, but he grimly hid the pain for fear he'd be benched.

Finally, he couldn't conceal it any longer. He had to be carried off the field, in agony.

The doctor took over, examined the boy and immediately got in touch with Coach Jones. "I hate to tell you this, Howard," he said with a sigh, "but your star guard's going to have to drop out of the lineup. Looks like he's been trying to ignore those injuries for some time. Now he's in pretty bad shape. I have to be honest with you. With a long rest, maybe he can make it for next season. And again, maybe he can't."

Coach Jones broke the news to Duke as gently as he could. "I want you back, Duke," he said. "We need you. But you've got to get a good rest and get well. The season's over now. Take it easy this summer, and probably by next fall you'll be in great shape again!"

Duke knew it wasn't possible for him to "take it easy." Working in a prop department isn't easy work, but there wasn't anything else he could do. At the end of the school year, he went back to 20th Century-Fox.

He hadn't been there long before John Ford found him. "Hear you're in trouble," he said quietly.

Duke smiled weakly and told him the story. There was something about this dour, taciturn man that, for some reason, seemed to enable everyone who worked for him to make him a trusted confidante. For one thing, he was a good listener.

After he'd heard Duke through he stood silently for a moment, thinking. Then he said, "Tell you what I think would be a good idea. Take a year off from school. I doubt if you can get those injuries healed in just a couple of months. It takes a lot of time. Don't worry about a job—you can go on working here. Then you can decide if you want to go back. A year isn't really so long."

"Thanks a lot," Duke said, "I guess I'd better do that."

Neither of them was kidding the other. They both knew that, in all probability, Duke wouldn't get that scholarship back. But for Duke, John Ford had salvaged something very important. His pride.

When he went back to work, Duke felt lost and confused. The future that had been so glowing just a few months before had vanished. True, he was making enough money to date Josephine. But what about the future? She couldn't marry a prop man!

As usual, John Ford was very much aware of this. In Janurary 1928, at a time when all his Sigma Chi frat brothers were having a great celebration of the holidays and Duke was walking disconsolately around the Fox lot carrying furniture, John Ford walked up to him and said casually, "I have a part for you."

"*Me*?" Duke asked incredulously.

"I've worked with worse slobs than you," Ford retorted. "Report to the assistant director tomorrow. He'll tell you what to do."

Could it be possible? Suddenly, the "acting" dreams, the games he'd played as a boy, came back to him. What fun it was! But that was kid stuff. He wasn't an actor. Why, he'd never even been to drama school or on the stage, like the actors who worked in the movies. He'd better forget it.

He went though with it, anyway. And as it turned out, it wasn't much. The picture was called *Hangman's House*, and all he had to do was stand in front of the judge with his head down while he received the sentence, "You shall hang by the neck until dead, dead, dead!"

Simple enough. But Duke learned, right there, that movies are made by repeating the "take" over and over, until everything is exactly right.

At about the tenth "take," after the words had been pronounced sentencing him to the gallows, he couldn't resist fervently adding, "Amen!"

"Get that imbecile off this set!" Ford roared. "I never want to see him again!"

To Duke it was the first time he realized that Ford's wrath could, indeed, be formidable. To Ford it was "the first time I got a real reaction out of him!"

Months went by, and Duke felt his chances of becoming an actor were over. Nobody offered him an acting job. He was resigned to being in the prop department forever. Then in 1929, the man who "never wanted to see him again" looked him up.

"Duke," John Ford said abruptly, "I'd like you to do me a favor."

In what was to become his standard reply throughout their lifetimes, Duke said, "Sure. What is it?"

Ford explained that he was to make a football film at Annapolis, and wanted to know if Duke could use his influence with the USC coach to get the team sprung from school for two weeks to do the football sequences. "I'll give you a part in the picture, too," Ford offered.

With Coach Jones on his side, pleading that the trip to Annapolis would be "an educational experience" for the team, the deal was made with the school authorities, and Duke found himself back in a football uniform for the picture titled *Salute*. Alas, he wasn't the big hero—that was George O'Brien, the star. But he did meet another bit player with whom he struck up an instant and lasting friendship. His name was Ward Bond.

The coming of sound had brought a heady atmosphere to Hollywood. Along with sound came the Big Picture, the super-extravaganza that was conceived to rival, or possibly surpass, the Seven Wonders of the World.

Such an epic was *The Big Trail*, planned by Fox for release in 1929, with glorious sound and a magnificent new film technique that would make the picture bigger, wider and three-dimensional.

The director assigned to the film was doughty Raoul Walsh. Like John Ford, Walsh was a hard-bitten pro who knew his business thoroughly and took no back talk from anyone.

Walsh confided to Ford that he was having trouble finding a leading man. He'd wanted Gary Cooper, but Paramount wouldn't let him go after the hit he'd made in *The Virginian*.

"I've got a fellow working on my lot who might interest you," Ford said. "Why don't you come and take a look at him?"

Walsh, who wore a patch over one eye, had the reputation of seeing with far greater penetration with one good eye than most people with two good eyes. When Duke noticed this man with the eyepatch hanging around the set for several days, he had a strange feeling that he was staring right through him. It made him nervous.

He was carrying a table across the lot when he

stumbled over a cable, landing right in front of Walsh. Luckily, the director escaped harm, but the table was completely demolished.

Walsh walked away, unperturbed. Later he told Ford, "I like the way that kid walks. I think I'll test him."

When he was called to Walsh's office, Duke was sure he was going to catch hell for the table incident. He was bowled over when Walsh told him that he planned to test him. "You'll remain on salary, but you won't work in the prop department. Just do what I tell you. Right now, you're going to learn to throw knives."

It sounded weird. This was *acting*? Nevertheless, he dutifully learned how to throw knives from a studio expert. It was easy.

Next, he was delivered into the hands of a teacher who was supposed to train him in voice and dramatics. This was a disaster.

In an all-out effort to cope with the problems of sound, the Hollywood studios had imported numerous teachers, mainly from New York, to give their contract players lessons in voice and dramatics. Unfortunately, not all of these teachers were as highly qualified as they should have been.

The teacher Duke got was of the old Shakespearean, sweeping-cape school, doting on wide gestures and rolling r's.

To Duke, all this seemed quite ridiculous. As far as his speech went, he did have a bit of a Midwestern twang dating from his Iowa childhood, but what was wrong with that? As for his language, his speech and articulation were as good as anybody's, and he had all those honor grades in high school and college to prove it. As for acting—well, if those phony gestures were what they wanted, they'd better count him out.

After six "lessons" the teacher threw in the towel, with a final dramatic pronouncement: "Young man, you'll never be an actor in a hundred years!"

Duke was ready to go back to the prop department when Walsh called him in again. All he said was, "I'm going to test you tomorrow."

Chapter 6

A STAR ISN'T BORN

"My debut in motion pictures wasn't exactly auspicious. At 20th Century-Fox, I starred in three bombs in succession. The second one, Girls Demand Excitement, *was unquestionably the worst motion picture ever made!"*

Duke was surprised, when he reported for the test, that it wasn't at all like he expected. "Thank God," he thought, "they aren't going to make me up." But they didn't give him a script to memorize, either. He was beginning to think it was all a gag, maybe a practical joke.

The stars who'd already been signed for *The Big Trail*, Ian Keith and Marguerite Churchill, were standing idly beside a covered wagon.

Suddenly, seemingly out of nowhere, Walsh appeared. "Okay, Duke," he said sharply, "you get in there with Keith and Marguerite. You're supposed to be the scout leader. Keith's going to throw questions at you, and you answer whatever comes into your head. That clear?"

"Y-yes," Duke answered uncertainly.

"Action!" called Walsh.

As the cameras turned, hapless Duke was caught in a crossfire of Keith's questions, thrown at him fast and furiously. At first, he attempted replies, but as the pace mounted, he became furious. What kind of test was this, anyway?

He turned on Keith and fired questions back. At the moment, he didn't give a damn whether the cameras were turning or not. He *was* the lead scout, putting down somebody who had no right to question his authority.

"Cut!" Walsh called. "Print it!"

"My big chance and I blew the whole thing," Duke thought ruefully.

What Raoul Walsh was thinking was very different. Even without seeing the test on film, he knew he had found his star. Duke had performed exactly as he had wanted him to.

A contract was drawn up, paying Duke seventy-five dollars a week. But when Raoul Walsh looked at the contract, he recoiled in horror.

"Marion!" he gasped. "Marion Michael Morrison!

Good God, whoever heard of a cowboy named Marion? We've got to do something about that!''

The great crisis reached the office of Winfield Sheehan, who was then head of production.

Duke agreed, wholeheartedly, that Marion was undesirable. What about Michael Morrison?

No. Too long, and anyway the public would shorten it to Mike which was associated with the Irish and would consequently alienate other ethnic groups.

"Okay. So how about Duke Morrison? Everybody calls me that, anyway."

Duke? It suggested royalty, which even in the wildest stretch of the imagination anyone could see that Duke wasn't.

At last Sheehan, in one of those bursts of brilliance for which production heads of studios collect their phenomenal salaries, came up with the perfect name—John Wayne.

It was beautiful. It was down-to-earth American, and wouldn't offend any ethnic group. Above all, it was short, so that it could be easily fitted on a marquee and still leave space for more important things, like "A 20th Century-Fox Production."

Duke didn't like the name change, but by this time he was so thoroughly oriented to movie-making that he understood the movie-makers' thinking.

He was also completely sold on becoming an actor. For one thing, he knew that if he made it there was a lot more money to be had than he could possibly make as a struggling young lawyer hanging out his shingle. And making money was the one way, he knew, that he could ever marry Josephine.

Of course, that wasn't sufficient motivation to guarantee success as an actor. What did guarantee it was the same quality that those experts, John Ford and Raoul Walsh, detected—the very rare ability to feel emotion in any given situation and express that feeling on the screen.

It would be pleasant to report that John Wayne's first starring movie, *The Big Trail*, was a big success.

The truth is that *The Big Trail* was a big flop.

This had nothing whatever to do with the new star's acting or the fact that he was an unknown. Not only was the acting unusually competent, but the whole concept of the film was unusually advanced.

In it, the producers had grasped one of the fundamentals of a successful Western—capturing the panorama of the vast, open spaces of the country—which has given every Western to this day the stamp of authenticity, as well as giving to audiences the feeling that they are being transported into that time and place.

They accomplished this to a greater degree than ever before with new camera techniques that had the effect of widening and deepening the screen. The picture had a grand, almost three-dimensional effect.

Not surprisingly, the mastermind behind this process, known as 70mm Grandeur, was Raoul Walsh.

Unfortunately, in November 1929, *The Big Trail* was preceded by The Big Crash. As the country's economy toppled, theater owners panicked along with the rest of the nation. They simply couldn't afford to put out the money for the special equipment the film required.

Faced with this disaster, Fox hastily released a regular 35 mm version. It didn't do much good.

Ironically, some twenty-five years later not only the same techniques but the same *cameras* were exhumed by 20th Century-Fox and, as CinemaScope, used with improved color film to produce *The Robe* and other big money-making hits.

If the movie-makers of *The Big Trail* were about a quarter of a century before their time, this was also true of their choice of a star, give or take some years.

Thoroughly discouraged, Duke moped around the lot. The reviews of his performance were hardly impressive.

He was wondering whether he should quit and go back to school when another Fox director, Seymour Felix, decided to team him and his *Big Trail* co-star, Marguerite Churchill, in a picture called *Girls Demand Excitement*.

"It was," Duke declared volubly whenever it was mentioned in future years, "unquestionably the worst picture that was ever made by the motion picture industry." In private company, he has been known to use much stronger language.

The unbelievable plot and dialogue reached a high point in a basketball game between a boys' team and a girls' team.

"God, did I hate making that picture," Duke said, then and now, and for all time.

Nevertheless, Fox put him into another of the cutesy, bird-brained concoctions that they, in their wisdom, were sure the public was dying to see. Titled *Three Girls Lost*, it was another bomb.

Unlike the other film, this one did have one saving grace in the presence of his lovely co-star, Loretta Young.

Fragile and beautiful as she appeared, Loretta was already a seasoned movie actress, having begun to act while in her early teens. She could—and did—give Duke many a helpful hint.

No, they didn't fall madly in love. On the contrary, Duke discovered that Loretta, like Josie, was a devout Catholic, and she was the one person to whom he could confide his marriage plans!

"How wonderful!" Loretta exclaimed. "Oh, Duke, I'd love to meet her!" Then, she added thoughtfully, "Maybe I could help her to understand your work. I hope so. . . ."

When Duke finished *Three Girls Lost*, he suffered the terrible fate of many an actor. His option wasn't picked up. Translated, that means that the clause in his contract providing for a renewal of his services was not exercised. In short, he was unemployed.

This doleful situation lasted exactly one week. Then he got an offer from Columbia Pictures.

As Duke was to learn through painful experience in the years to come, Columbia was not doing this because they were bowled over by his talent. They were simply shrewd enough to grab him and go for a quick cash-in from all the publicity and build-up investment that had been made by Fox.

In those days, Columbia Pictures was ruled with an iron hand—fist might be a better word—by Harry Cohn, head of studio production.

Duke got a great education from Harry Cohn while

grinding out three films for him—*Arizona, Range Feud* and *Maker of Men*. From Cohn he learned, firsthand, about everything that was wrong with the movie industry.

Cohn's reputation throughout his long tenure at Columbia was that of a clever, wily, utterly ruthless and unscrupulous despot. Throughout the industry, he could have won any unpopularity contest, hands down. Behind his back, he was seldom referred to by his given name but almost invariably as "that son-of-a-bitch."

By this time, Duke had acquired a reputation, too. He was regarded as an affable, easy going guy who worked hard, liked a good laugh, could drink anybody under the table, and had an appreciative eye for women. He also had a hot temper when it was aroused.

Inevitably, Harry Cohn aroused it. One day Cohn, who demanded lily-white moral standards of his contract players (which, of course, did not apply to himself), called Duke into his office. Though the exact words exchanged were not recorded for posterity, it must have gone something like this:

Cohn: "You've been boozing on the set and screwing around with your leading ladies and I want it stopped immediately!"

Duke (coming to a slow boil): "That's a pretty rough accusation. I think I have a right to ask how you dare to make it."

Cohn (flustered by this unheard-of back talk, shuffles through the papers on his desk and grabs a few at random): "Evidence! Evidence! I've got it right here!"

Duke rises to his six-foot-four height and glares down at Cohn. "Listen, you f____ son-of-a-bitch," he says evenly, "I don't give a good goddamn what trumped-up 'evidence' you have. Sure, I like to take a drink and I like women. What do you think I am, a fairy? But I don't booze or play around on the set. And what I do off the set is none of your f_____ business!''

And with that, he probably turned and left the room.

After he'd simmered down, Duke tried to figure out Cohn's motives.

True, there'd been a lot of rumors going around about him and Susan Fleming who'd been his leading lady in *Range Feud*. Susan was a sultry type and he did find her attractive, but it was nothing serious. After all, he was engaged to Josie. In any case, such ''romance rumors'' were all to the good as far as the picture was concerned. Rumors like this were often made up by press agents to hype interest in a picture.

He had to conclude—as many people who worked for Cohn had already concluded—that this was simply a browbeating technique, a means Cohn used to keep players knuckling under to his complete domination.

Well, Duke knew, he hadn't knuckled under. And he wasn't sorry. He also wasn't surprised when Columbia dropped him after he finished *Maker of Men*.

Characteristically, Harry Cohn got his revenge by dropping that bomb just when it would hurt the most—on Christmas Eve.

Thoroughly disillusioned by his experience at Columbia, Duke seriously considered giving up acting. At the beginning of 1932, he was still young enough to go back to USC, play football and get that law degree. But that would mean another long wait before he and Josie could get married.

Then, too, although he'd come to know the seamy

side of the movie industry—the crass anything-to-make-a-buck side—he'd met some fine, talented and dedicated people, too. People like John Ford, with whom he could share his own growing feeling that movie-making could be something much more important than cheap entertainment.

Immediately, he had to face one fact—he was out of a job. Even if he did go back to school, he'd have to work until fall.

When Sid Rogell, head of Mascot Productions, offered him the lead in a series called *Shadow of the Eagle*, he jumped at it, even though it was "cheap entertainment" in every sense of the word. Mascot was one of those small companies that were springing up like mushrooms along with what the big studios called Poverty Row. They ground out movies like hamburger.

Before he signed Duke, Sid asked, "Are you a drinking man?"

"Sure," Duke said cheerfully.

"Er—I mean—well, do you drink on the set or fool around with broads?"

Suddenly, the light dawned. "Why, that lousy, f_____, rotten son-of-a-bitch!" Duke exploded. "He's behind this, isn't he?"

Rogell burst out laughing. Then he held out a pen. "Here," he said, "Sign it."

Duke did, but not before telling Rogell that he intended to separate Harry Cohn from a certain part of his anatomy and immortalize said part in the cement of Grauman's Chinese Theatre.

If Duke had known that he was going to go on galloping as a Horse Opera Hero for the next seven years, he might have faded off into the sunset right there. But the work was pleasant. He always did like to ride. And the pay was good—$150 a week was a lot of money in those days.

Following the *Shadow of the Eagle* series, he made at least thirteen westerns by the spring of 1933, an incredible record. He made them for all comers, big studios and small, and even threw in a couple for his old arch-enemy, Harry Cohn. Yes, hard-hearted Harry, as usual, was willing to let bygones be bygones when he saw the money that was coming in from Duke's low-budgeted efforts for Mascot and others.

Naturally, Duke's breakneck pace had a motivation. By the spring of 1933, he was finally able to ask Josephine Saenz to marry him!

Unknown to Duke, another tremendous event in his life was beginning to shape up at about the same time.

One day, while reading an issue of *Collier's* magazine, John Ford found a short story titled "Last Stage to Lordsburg."

It struck him that the story had all the elements of a good movie Western.

He took it to Dudley Nichols, one of Hollywood's very best screenwriters.

"What do you think, Dudley?" he asked. "I think it would make a hell of a movie."

Nichols read it and agreed. "I'll do the screenplay for you," he said.

"Fine," said Ford. "Go right ahead."

He had turned to go, when Nichols called after him, "Oh, by the way, Jack, who do you see as the lead in this? I know it's none of my business. I'm just curious.

But maybe it'll help me if I know who you've got in mind.''

"John Wayne," said Ford.

"John *who*?" Nichols wasn't quite sure he'd heard right.

"Never mind," said Ford, "just go ahead and write the script."

Nichols turned in his usual expert job on the script, and John Ford began to peddle it to producers. All of them loved it.

"Now, let's see," they'd say. "We'll have to get a really big name star. Maybe Gary Cooper or Clark Gable . . ."

"No," Ford would reply quietly. "I've already picked my star. John Wayne."

The reaction was always the same. "Jack, whoever heard of John Wayne? It's a great script but, damn it, no producer in his right mind is going to risk that kind of bankroll on an unknown!"

And Ford would just pick up his script and leave. This went on for *five years!*

Chapter 7

JOSIE—FROM BLISS TO BOREDOM

"She's a fine girl and a really wonderful mother. But it was best for both of us to part. There is no bitterness between us. We respect each other. Our relationship is pleasant . . ."

———————————◆◆◆◆◆———————————

In June of 1933, Duke and Josephine Saenz were married. It was a beautiful wedding in the garden of Loretta Young's home, and she was thrilled to be a bridesmaid.

The guests were an odd mixture of Duke's not-so-

social family, his rather raucous movie-making cronies and Josephine's family and friends, who were strictly high society.

Sweetly diplomatic Loretta, who was completely at ease with all factions, managed the whole affair very smoothly. Ever since Duke had confided his love for Josie to her when they were making *Three Girls Lost*, Loretta had become a trusted friend to both of them— and would remain so through all the years to come.

Knowing the movie business as she did, Loretta couldn't help having a few misgivings about the match. She knew the demands of Duke's work would be very hard for Josie to understand. "But they're so in love," she thought. And wasn't that supposed to conquer everything?

Nobody could have told the blissful couple anything then—especially that there is no such thing as love at first sight. It had happened to them!

They first met in September 1926 when Duke had returned to USC for his second year. With money in his pocket from working in the Fox prop department all summer, he was finally able to indulge in a little social life. So, when one of his frat pals at Sigma Chi (where he no longer had to wash dishes for his meals) asked him to go along on a blind date with "a real beaut named Carmen," he accepted enthusiastically.

Carmen Saenz lived up to his expectations. She was lovely and charming, and the four of them had a lot of fun.

When he took Carmen home, he was a bit bowled over by the elegant, richly furnished living room they entered. But that was nothing compared to the way he was bowled over by the sight of Carmen's younger sister, Josephine.

Josie had just come home with her date, so Duke lost no time in making a suggestion that the four of them run down to Balboa for a snack. Once they got there, he lost no time in maneuvering Josie out on the pier nearby, for "a look at the ocean."

Maybe Josie was feeling the same way Duke was because she accepted readily enough. There was something very different about this boy that set him apart from all the rich society boys she'd been dating . . . a kind of strength, and he seemed so sincere.

Standing on the Balboa pier with the moonlight casting its spell on the Pacific, they didn't say anything. Duke drew Josie into his arms, and the kiss they exchanged said it all.

From that moment, Duke knew that for the first time in his life, he had fallen deeply in love. He decided then and there to make Josephine his wife.

But he was in no position to get married. There he was, a poor college boy who had hardly enough to support himself, let alone a wife! Well, he wasn't going to let it get him down. He'd get that law degree, hang out his shingle and they'd settle down in a cozy little house.

Of course, he took it for granted that Josie would accept him. Not that he thought he was anything so great, but she just *had* to! If he had to move heaven and earth, he was going to win that girl!

He didn't exactly move heaven and earth, but during the next seven years his efforts to win the love of his life rivaled those of the Biblical Jacob, who toiled for seven years to win his Rachel.

Unlike Jacob, fortunately, Duke didn't have to toil

for seven years. In fact, he wouldn't have had to knock himself out making all those Grade D westerns. Josie, impressed by his hard-working dedication, realized that there was, indeed, a big difference between Duke and the wealthy idlers she'd known. Another thing—he wasn't a phony. When he told her he loved her, she knew he meant it. That thrilled her even more than his bright blue eyes, his lop-sided smile and the warm, protected feeling she had when he put his arms around her and pulled her against his chest. She'd have married him any time.

Any spats they had were about money. She couldn't understand why it was so important to him. Raised in luxury, it had never been a problem for her.

Duke stuck to his guns—and to his saddle. Like Josie, he had been brought up in the Roman Catholic faith and he had very strong ideas about marriage. A husband should be able to provide for his wife and future family. Until he felt sure that he was able to do that, they couldn't marry.

He dated Josie whenever he could, and after a while they became formally engaged. It was all very proper.

Being a red-blooded young man, he couldn't help being attracted by some of the pretty actresses he met on the set, and from time to time rumors circulated that he had "a big, hot romance" going with this one or that one.

Sometimes this was the work of overzealous press agents trying to hype interest in the movie he was making with fake "romance" items. This was a common practice in Hollywood.

In any event, he managed to convince Josie that the rumors were "nothing at all."

Throughout their courtship, Josie had seen only the

glamorous side of Duke's work—the name "John Wayne" on theater marquees, the excitement of seeing him on the screen.

"That doesn't mean a thing, Josie," he'd scoff. "Making movies is just a lot of hard work."

She thought he was being modest and loved him for it.

He was simply telling the truth. At the pace he was working, his sheer physical efforts alone were equivalent to those of an entire U.S. Olympic team.

When they were finally married and settled down in a nice, furnished apartment, Duke had to go right back to the movie-making grind to keep that $150 a week coming in.

He left the house at five o'clock in the morning, to face a day that might include long gallops in the dust and scorching sun, a couple of fist fights that, even with pulled punches, had to look convincing, and a few barroom brawls. Of course, all of this had to be done over and over until the director got a good "take."

Only a person with an exceptionally strong physique could have taken this punishment. Duke had it, but he wasn't Superman and when he finally got hime, never before 7:30, he was exhausted. All he wanted to do was take a hot shower, enjoy a good dinner, relax for a little while with his wife, and get some sleep before the alarm went off at 5:00 A.M.

But Josie had other ideas. Chances were that Josie had accepted a dinner invitation from one of her friends. She'd have his dinner clothes all ready. "It'll be fun, Duke," she'd tell him. "You'll like them."

Maybe he would have if he hadn't had to concentrate so much on keeping his eyes open all evening. But if it made Josie happy . . .

This social whirl came to a merciful end when Josie became pregnant, and in 1934 their first child, a son, was born. He looked a lot like his proud father, and they named him—naturally—Michael.

It would have been hard to find two happier, more devoted parents than Duke and Josie. With this new responsibility, Duke worked harder than ever. From the beginning, Josie was an ideal mother.

Duke was still galloping away through oat operas for anyone who'd hire him when he was approached by Herbert Yates. Yates, one of the more farsighted of Hollywood's masterminds, had gathered together several tottering studios on Poverty Row, including Monogram Studios, where Duke was currently employed, and formed Republic Pictures. Since Duke had a contract with Monogram, he went along with the deal.

He was happy about it. He knew the move put Yates in a position to make bigger, more expensive movies. Sure enough, it wasn't long before Yates called him and told him he was to star in a Republic extravaganza titled *Westward, Ho!*, to be made with the magnificent budget of $17,000!

The picture, directed by Robert N. Bradbury, was finished in about three weeks. Released in August 1935, it grossed $500,000 by the end of the year. To Duke, the only benefit of this thirty-to-one payoff was that throughout the country the press began to really take notice of John Wayne.

It followed that Republic was eager to cash in on this great bonanza. As in the case of *The Big Trail*, unlucky Duke was to become the victim of advanced thinking on the part of his employers.

By 1935, the Hollywood musical was in full sway,

complete with Busby Berkeley chorus girls, the most expensive sets and the most expensive tunesmiths in show business, including George and Ira Gershwin.

What could be better than combining that hit formula, the Western, with music?

For Republic, chorus girls, expensive talent and sets were out. They figured they could get the same effect from an appealing, guitar-strumming, singing cowboy.

As they had a new star of their hands, anyway, as a result of *Westward Ho!*, why not cash in on it?

A new series, titled *Singin' Sandy*, got under way, starring John Wayne. In the movie, Duke was supposed to go through his usual paces, plus twanging a fake guitar and warbling a few Western ditties.

There were a couple of things wrong with this admirable idea: (1) Duke couldn't sing. (2) He couldn't play the guitar.

In the first opus, Duke did his own singing, if you could call it that. Actually, he sort of hummed while plunking away on the fake guitar with hands that resembled catcher's mitts.

He did the same in the second opus except that the producers had wisely decided that he shouldn't sing; his voice should be dubbed.

Duke had found out that Bradbury had employed his son and friends to provide the musical effects. Duke decided that this had to end. He told Republic to go find themselves another singing cowboy. Most of all, they'd made him feel like a goddamn phony, trying to pretend he could sing and play the guitar when he couldn't.

Very sensibly, Yates took Duke's advice. He hired a young fellow who *could* sing and play the guitar. His name was Gene Autry.

Gratefully, Duke went back to the rough-and-tumble Westerns. He'd rather go through ten barroom brawls than plunk that fake guitar.

It wasn't such a bad deal, anyway. He'd worked his way up to $4,000 per picture; they look less than two months to shoot and he was working constantly. Sure, the pictures looked as if they'd come off an assembly line, but it was a good living—plenty to support his family.

A growing family it was, too. His first daughter, a dark-haired darling who looked like her mother, was born in 1936 and named Antonia Maria, soon shortened to Toni.

In 1938, a second son, Patrick, arrived. By this time, Duke had a new contract with Universal Pictures for $6,000 per picture. He'd been delighted not only with the money but the chance to do non-Western films. The first, *The Sea Spoilers*, was an adventure on the bounding waves that he thoroughly enjoyed.

Josie wasn't enjoying it so much. The financial security was fine, but with Duke's increasing prestige, he wasn't making quickie movies in back lots anymore. More and more, he was off on long location trips while she stayed in the nursery.

When does a marriage begin to fall apart?

Sometimes it happens with a few tremors, followed by an earthquake shock that leaves nothing but torn shreds of emotion. More often it is a slow corrosion, an almost imperceptible crumbling that gives no hint of the destruction to come.

That was the way it was for Duke and Josie.

From the outset, both had made a real effort to reconcile their very different backgrounds. Duke dutifully got himself duded up and dragged himself to the parties of Josie's society friends, feeling as out of place as Toots Shor at an afternoon tea.

On her part, Josie insisted that he invite his pals to their home. He did—but even with Josie tactfully retiring, her ladylike presence put a damper on their usual roistering, bottle-sharing, poker-playing fun. Even such stalwarts as John Ford and Ward Bond began to suggest that they get together elsewhere.

From the time their first baby was born, the bond between Josie and Duke subtly changed from love for each other to love for the children they both adored.

They thought it was enough. They didn't know that between a man and a woman it never is.

When Duke began to go away on long location trips, the separation that had been a not-too-serious one of tastes and personalities became an actual, physical one.

He'd come home, arms loaded with gifts, and smother them all with bear hugs and kisses. Once more, his warmth and booming laughter would fill the house that seemed so empty without him. Once more, everything was all right.

Then he'd have to leave again. The emptiness would come back. And a lonely Josie, with only their small children for company, couldn't help but wonder what kind of company Duke was keeping.

Though neither of them could possibly realize it at the time, the year 1938 marked the beginning of the end of their marriage.

That was the year when John Wayne, hitherto regarded as a clod who plodded his way through sagebrush sagas, came into his own a star of the first rank.

Unknown to Duke, his friend John Ford was still

peddling the script of *Stagecoach* to producers, with the stipulation that the star had to be John Wayne.

Once, he casually handed Duke the script and asked him to read it.

"Good script," Duke told him when he handed it back at their next poker-playing session. "Real good."

"I thought so," Ford said, shuffling the cards and taking a sip from his drink. "Who do you think would be good to play the Ringo Kid?"

"Well, let's see." Duke thought for a moment. "I know. Lloyd Nolan. He'd be fine!"

Ford threw down his cards in disgust. "Oh, you dumb son-of-a-bitch," he shouted. "Can't you see that *you're* the Ringo Kid?"

Duke grinned and shook his head. "They won't give it to me. You know that, Jack. Not in a million years."

Finally, in 1939, Ford decided to show the script to Walter Wanger, who had become one of the industry's leading independent producers. He had a reputation as a man who would take a flyer on something offbeat if he thought the idea was good.

Along with other producers, Wanger was well aware that John Ford could make a poor script look a whole lot better and make a good script an outstanding hit.

Stagecoach was a good script. As for that Wayne fellow Jack insisted on having, it was probably worth taking a chance.

"I may be crazy, Jack," he told Ford. "I don't know anything about this Wayne and the part calls for a top star. But I trust your judgment. We'll do it."

The ink on the contracts was hardly dry when Ford was on the phone to Duke, shouting jubilantly, "Hey, you dumb son-of-a-bitch! You're the Ringo Kid!"

Ironically, shortly before shooting started on the picture that would be his son's great triumph, Clyde Morrison died of a heart attack. Just as success had eluded him in life, he was denied the satisfaction of his son's success.

At the time, Duke didn't know this. He only knew that he had lost a father who was "good and kind, and never had a harsh word for anyone. I owe him a great deal, and only hope I can live up to his example."

Stagecoach went into production early in 1939. For Duke the first couple of days on the set were sheer misery.

John Ford—his old pal, his buddy who'd fought to get him the part—turned on him savagely. Ford was known to his players as a tough taskmaster, but they'd never seen anything like it. Everything Duke did was wrong.

"Get the lead out of those feet, you clumsy bum!" Ford would bellow. "You walk like a drunken hippo! Maybe that gets by in those third-raters you've been making, but not here!"

When it came to acting, it was even worse. "Cut!" Ford would yell before Duke had even finished a sentence. "Tell me, do you have only one expression? That face of yours has about as much feeling in it as a death mask. When you smile, it looks like it's going to crack!"

By the end of two days of this constant baiting, everybody on the set was incensed on Duke's behalf, including his fellow *Stagecouch* passengers—Claire Trevor, Thomas Mitchell, John Carradine, George Bancroft and Andy Devine.

All their sympathy couldn't cheer Duke up. He felt he was a terrible failure and, worst of all, he'd failed John Ford's faith in him.

By the third day, he'd decided that he'd better go to Ford, make his apologies and get out of the picture before it was too late. He could always go back to Republic Westerns.

Before he got a chance to make his little speech, Ford came up behind him. "Don't worry about anything, Duke," he said in a low voice the others couldn't hear. "You're damn good!"

From then on, the pressure eased. Ford continued to crack the whip, but not so hard.

Ford had watched the rushes of the first two days' shooting intently. There was Duke, playing the part of a tough young cowboy accused of his father's murder who'd broken out of jail to pursue the real killers.

In the opening scene, the passengers ask him who he is. "The Ringo Kid," he drawls. "That's what they call me. But my right name's Henry."

"I knew it! I knew it!" Ford thought happily. "That big, lovable bum has a way of making you *believe* in everything he does and says. He's going to be the biggest star this business has ever seen!"

As usual, John Ford was right. When *Stagecoach* was released late in 1939, John Wayne became an "overnight" sensation—after ten years of toiling in at least sixty films (he never could remember exactly how many).

Stagecoach was a tremendous success all around, winning not only laurels from the critics but a big payoff at the box office. Now firmly enshrined as one of the great classic Westerns of all time, it's still paying off handsomely in special releases and on TV.

With everything going so well, Duke, who never did hold a grudge, quickly forgot about the first days of agony that had brought him to the point of walking out.

John Ford didn't forget. He felt guilty about it. A long time afterward, he made a confession to Duke.

"I had to do it, Duke," he told him. "For one thing, I had to put you on your mettle, right from the start, so you wouldn't fall into any lazy habits you might've acquired from all those awful oaters you'd been making. Another thing—you were playing with a bunch of real top-drawer pros who could have resented the fact that I was bringing in somebody of less than top-star rank in a leading role. After two days of that beating I gave you, I had them all on your side!"

"Why, you no-good, low-down bastard!" Duke retorted. Then his face broke into a wide grin, and the two of them burst out laughing and went off to have a few drinks to celebrate the "confession."

To Duke, his elevation to top stardom was impressive in only two ways. He made a lot more money, and he didn't have to work so hard.

To Josie, happy and proud of her husband's success, it meant the same thing. Now, maybe Duke would have more time for her and the family.

It didn't work out that way. In the wake of *Stagecoach* came a couple of other high-budget Westerns, both teaming him again with Claire Trevor— *Allegheny Uprising* for RKO and *Dark Command* back at Republic. The latter film was highly successful financially and, in a sense, repaid the man who gave him his first big break—the director was Raoul Walsh.

Meanwhile, Republic was cashing in on the *Stagecoach* success by quickly releasing the Westerns Duke had made long before he started it—movies that were still in the can.

Duke could see what was happening, and he was disturbed at being typed forever as a hero on horseback. So was his friend, John Ford, who, as usual managed to come up with a solution.

"I'm going to do this picture, Duke," he said. "It's based on some plays by Eugene O'Neill. The main character is a Swedish sea captain. That's you."

"*Me?* A Swedish sea captain?" Duke exploded. "You've got to be out of your mind. Anyway, I can't do that O'Neill stuff. I'm not good enough. Go get some high-class actor."

"You *are* good enough," Ford insisted, "and you're going to do it!"

The Long Voyage Home was hailed as one of the finest films released in 1940, or any other year, for that matter. Again, Duke lived up to Ford's expectations. And the highest praise of all came from Eugene O'Neill himself who said it was the only film based on his work of which he completely approved.

Shortly after that triumph, another happy event occurred. On December 3, 1940, Duke and Josie were overjoyed when another baby girl arrived. They named her Melinda.

Now, they had a beautifully balanced family—two girls, two boys.

Unhappily, their marriage was becoming more and more unbalanced.

Instead of spending more time with his family, Duke was spending more time away from home. In part, it was due to the increased location-trip demands of the films he was making. It was also due to his own desire to enjoy life as he hadn't been able to do for years. He went on hunting and fishing trips, played poker, or just shot the breeze and passed a bottle with such movie-making cronies as John Ford, Ward Bond, Yakima Canutt ("the best stuntman in the business. He taught me how to fall off a galloping horse without getting hurt, and lots more"), Harry Carey—his boyhood idol—and Harry's son, Dobie, plus some other good people the public never heard of who worked behind the cameras.

Meanwhile, Josie was happily occupied with the children and her own friends, and the couple might have drifted along on this together-but-separate life style indefinitely had it not been for the rumors linking Duke with glamorous Marlene Dietrich. The gossip had started when the two were co-starred in *Seven Sinners* in 1940, and it got a lot hotter when they were paired again in *Pittsburgh* in 1942.

Josie, it was reported, also got a lot hotter. Whatever the facts were, stories were circulated that the Wayne marriage was definitely on the wane. In the usual Hollywood mixture of truths, half truths and pure conjecture, the stories ranged from picturing Duke and Josie in all-out battles to reporting that they had no arguments at all.

Through all this mishmash, one thing was clear. The "ideal" Wayne marriage *was* in bad trouble.

By the end of 1943, word had leaked out that it was all over. Still, there was nothing official. And apparently, the Marlene Dietrich episode—if there had been one—was a thing of the past.

Perhaps the problems might have blown over, if Duke hadn't decided to go to Mexico City with his friends Ward Bond, Fred MacMurray and Ray Milland to investigate buying a studio there to set up an independent film company. The deal didn't succeed. But a Mexican movie actress, Esperanza Bauer, succeeded in charming Duke right out of his mind.

Duke went to New Guinea from Mexico City on one of the many trips he made during the wartime years on behalf of the USO. As a father of four, he was exempt from active duty, but he did whatever he could to support the war effort.

Josie's chilly reception on his return should have tipped him off. She had heard about his gay evenings of nightclubbing in Mexico City with Esperanza.

They had it out and agreed that for the sake of the children, they'd try to make a go of it. Duke agreed to forget Esperanza if Josie would.

Josie wouldn't—and, possibly, Duke couldn't. At any rate, the "truce" was a short-lived, dismal failure.

If a divorce can possibly be called friendly, the word applies to that of Duke and Josie. Without the slightest hesitation, he handed over to her the custody of the children, their home and a fifth of his first $100,000 gross income a year, plus 10 percent of everything above that. In most years that was to amount to at least $60,000 a year.

"I gave her everything but the car," Duke said, "but

I'm glad to do it. She has the burden of raising the children, and she deserves every bit of it.''

Strangely, through the years to come, Duke and Josie got to know each other better than they ever had during their ten years of marriage. There were four good reasons—Michael, Toni, Patrick and Melinda. Duke was the first person Josie called if one of them became ill. Together, they discussed all the weighty problems of parents, such as whether Michael needed glasses or Melinda braces on her teeth.

Between them—not through the courts—a happy arrangement was worked out so that the children could spend summer vacations with their father wherever he might be.

It set a pattern he would follow always—having as many of his loved ones around him as possible, visiting or working with him. Perhaps it was because, deep inside, he realized that lack of closeness had cost him his first great love.

''I really didn't ever do anything wrong,'' he once said wistfully, ''except maybe stay away from home too long. But I thought I was doing the right thing then. That's no good for any marriage. Josephine and I simply drifted apart.''

Chapter 8

CHATA—TOO HOT NOT TO COOL DOWN

"It wasn't all bad. We had a lot of fun at first. But my name on that marriage license is one autograph I wish I hadn't signed!"

It's said that a man who experiences a great love that ends tends to fall in love again with the same type of woman.

Like Josephine Saenz, Esperanza Bauer was tall, dark, slim and Latin.

There, any resemblance ended.

Josephine was cool as a bowl of sherbert, reserved, quiet and always ladylike.

Esperanza was hot as a bowl of chili, uninhibited and vocal, and could hardly be described as a lady by any of the accepted standards.

At thirty, she had worked her way up through the cheap, shoddy world of Mexican film-making to a point where she had become a leading actress in south-of-the-border films. She had just finished the Spanish version of *The Count of Monte Cristo*, starring with Arturo De Cordova, when she met Duke.

Everybody called her Chata—roughly translated from the Mexican slang, "sweet little pugnose." When she smiled her wide, warm smile, her small nose crinkled and her black eyes snapped. The effect was altogether enchanting.

To say that Duke was enchanted would be putting it much too mildly. Whenever he experienced any emotion, it was roughly equivalent to a minor nuclear explosion.

Just why Chata had such an effect on him when they met in Mexico City wasn't hard to figure out.

At this point he and Josie had drifted so far apart that nothing could have got them back together again. At the same time, he was experiencing something he hadn't known in many years—freedom from the burden of working every day, year-in and year-out, to support himself and his family. Freedom to relax and enjoy life.

Now he was a top star, and even with the hefty payments he had to give Josephine, he didn't have to make more than a couple of pictures a year.

He continued to turn out what had become standard

John Wayne money-makers, in which he was either a wartime hero (*The Fighting Seabees, Back to Bataan, They Were Expendable*) or a horseback hero (*Tall in the Saddle, Flame of the Barbary Coast, Dakota*).

This took him into 1945 when, after fifteen years of continuous movie-making, he turned in his GI helmet and boots, his Stetson, chaps and spurs, and called it quits—at least for a while. He didn't make another movie for almost a year. To other stars who'd "made it big" this wasn't unusual. They usually paced themselves at one picture a year, or two at the most. For John Wayne it was unheard of. For him, four pictures a year was a leisurely rate.

Calm as he appeared on the outside, the breakup of his marriage to Josie had been a shattering blow. Since at last he could afford to take a long vacation, no one could blame him for wanting to go off and have fun and try to recover.

Those who knew him best realized there was another important reason for his "temporary retirement." No matter how often he was assured that the movies he made about the war were doing a much better job of contributing to education and morale than he could possibly have contributed in the armed forces, he felt it wasn't enough. He had been doing whatever he could—visiting the troops at home and abroad, appearing at bond rallies—but too often (to suit him) such requests had conflicted with movie schedules. He wanted to make himself available whenever needed.

Of course, when he wasn't busy on such assignments he lost no time in getting together with Chata.

To say that she caught him on the rebound wouldn't be quite fair. She happened to have some very attractive qualities that Duke had not found in other women.

It wasn't just physical appeal. Duke had been exposed to plenty of fabulous beauties in Hollywood. Chata, with her upturned nose and rather coarse Mexican features, probably wouldn't be regarded as a great beauty. But then Duke never considered himself any prize in that respect.

One important factor that drew them together was similar backgrounds. Both had worked to top star status in movies the hard way. In Chata, Duke felt he'd at last found a woman who could really understand him and his work.

Most importantly, Chata filled a void, a need of a man who, for the first time, found himself lonely.

She was a good-time girl who loved to go out on the town until the wee hours of the morning. She loved to dance, all dressed up in pretty, feminine gowns, but wasn't above having a few drinks and laughing heartily at off-color jokes. And if she didn't particularly enjoy hunting and fishing expeditions, she was game enough to go along and pretend she did.

After months of this happy relationship, Duke and Chata finally decided to get a marriage license.

The wedding posed a few problems. Both were divorced. (Chata had had a brief marriage in 1941, lasting not even a year, to a man named, oddly enough, Eugene Morrison). Yet they wanted a church wedding with a few attendants and a small reception. Considering Duke's recent divorce, a large affair would have been in bad taste—and he had previously been married in the Roman Catholic Church.

To the rescue, as always, came Duke's mother. Several years after his father's death, Molly Morrison had married a man named Sidney Preen, who her son described as "a wonderful guy." They were happily settled in Long Beach.

Molly, who reveled in her role of grandmother to Duke's children, had been saddened by his divorce. But having gone through one marriage and subsequently finding happiness with someone else, Molly only hoped that her son would be so fortunate.

Briskly, she went about making the arrangements and on January 17, 1946, Duke and Chata were married at the United Presbyterian Church in Long Beach. Duke's good friend, Ward Bond, was best man. Olie Carey, wife of another of his best friends, Harry Carey, who had passed away, was matron of honor. The ceremony was held with a minimum of fanfare, and Molly invited everyone to a lovely reception at her home.

Duke and Chata settled down in a $125,000, twenty-two room mansion in the San Fernando Valley, and Chata lost no time in filling its closets with a wardrobe befitting John Wayne's wife. She also installed a new fixture—her mother.

This didn't bother Duke, as there was plenty of room for the three of them to rattle around in. Besides, it saved money on phone bills because every time Mama went back to Mexico City Chata phoned her constantly.

Duke was away from home much of the time, anyway. He had to be; he had to keep up with his rapidly mounting expenses. Early in 1946, he made one of his few comedies, *Without Reservations*, at RKO. Under the direction of Mervyn LeRoy, a comedy expert, and co-starring Claudette Colbert and Don Defore, it was a hit. But Duke was never comfortable out of the saddle too long, so he chose as his next film a Western, *Angel and the Badman*, back on the old Republic lot.

It wasn't among his best movies, but it had farreaching effects on his own life and that of his co-star, Gail Russell.

Chata was convinced that they were playing love scenes for real. Though Duke had been teamed with many beauties in movies, for some reason—perhaps her woman's instincts—Chata became insanely jealous of Gail.

One incident that really fanned the flames was the rumor that Duke had given Gail a car.

"'Ow can you do thees to me?'' Chata screamed. ''I am your wife, and you geeve her a car!''

''I *didn't* give her a car,'' Duke protested wearily. ''She needed a car to get to work and didn't have the money, so I loaned her the down payment.''

The explanation didn't quell Chata's suspicions. They exploded like a ton of TNT on the night of the party celebrating the end of shooting on the picture.

In Hollywood, such parties are a tradition. Friends and relatives aren't invited, but everyone who worked on the movie, from the stars to the lowliest grips, gets together for an uproarious good time after their months of hard work.

Chata understood this. What she couldn't understand was why her husband failed to come home.

She and her mother had a few drinks to calm their nerves. Pacing the floor, Chata raged, ''He is weeth that woman! I weel show him!''

She phoned Gail's house. Later, she swore that someone there gave her the number of a motel in the Valley. Since Gail lived alone with her mother, this didn't seem likely. It could have been a wrong number. Whatever it was, it had an explosive effect on Chata.

"He weel not get away with thees!" she stormed, running around and locking all the doors.

Exhausted from their strenuous evening, she and her mother went to bed.

Somewhere between 4:00 and 5:00 A.M., there was a loud crash, followed by sounds of falling glass.

Still somewhat woozy, Chata grabbed one of the guns she and Duke used on their hunting trips. She headed downstairs, Mama behind her.

In the dark, Chata could make out a large body on the sofa. She aimed straight at it.

"No, no!" Mama shouted, grabbing the gun. "Eet ees your 'usband!"

It was. Finding the door locked—and not finding his key—Duke had kicked in the glass to open the door. Then, after the night's revelries, he fell asleep on the nearest sofa.

Sobered by the thought that she might have killed him, Chata was ready to make up with Duke. She was certain that it was a burglar who had broken in, she said. He told her that yes, he had stopped at Gail's house, but it was just to have a couple of nightcaps with her and her mother after the party. Then he came home and broke in when he couldn't find his key.

The incident shored up the shaky Wayne marriage for a while. Both Duke and Chata appeared to be making an effort to keep it intact. As before, they went on location and on outdoor vacations together in an attempt to recapture the fun-filled intimacy of their first meetings.

Unfortunately, as they went the "fun" route, Chata

made an effort to keep up with her husband in drinking—an attempt similar to that of a Girl Scout trying to scale Mt. Everest. Strong men had been known to quail, confronted by Big Duke's capacity for the cup that cheers.

The rumors started again—ugly rumors of drunken brawls between them at parties and in nightclubs.

The Iron Duke—as his friends began to call him— didn't let any of this interfere with his work. Two of his finest films—*Fort Apache*, for his old friend, John Ford, and *Red River*, directed by Henry Hathaway— were made during this period, plus a couple of lesser efforts.

That was fine with Chata, until she heard about his next picture, *Wake of the Red Witch*. His co-star was to be Gail Russell.

With her Mexican blood boiling, Chata packed and, with Mama in tow, headed for Mexico City.

The rest of the alliance of Duke and Chata was prolonged agony. Though *Wake of the Red Witch* was completed without any blowups about Gail, there were fights and reconciliations, more fights and more reconciliations.

When Chata took to confiding to reporters: "He ees a terrible man. He beats me up all thee time. I weel leave heem! Deevorce heem!" it didn't help matters.

Duke stayed away from home much of the time and buried his troubles in work. He also needed the money—badly. Though he was now pulling down $150,000 per picture, it was going out as fast as he earned it—for taxes, agents' fees, his obligations to Josie and the children, and maintaining Chata and her mother in the style to which they had become accustomed.

When he did come home it was a dismal scene, with the three of them moping around the big house, not speaking to each other.

In November 1951, he couldn't take it anymore. He packed his bags and flew to Acapulco, leaving a note for Chata: "If you want to see me, you know where you can find me . . ." They had been happy there, once.

She didn't come. As Christmas neared, Duke decided to make one more attempt to let bygones be bygones. He came back to the Encino home, laden with Christmas presents, including one for Mama.

The Christmas spirit hadn't gotten through to Chata and Mama. After a brief visit with his children, Duke went back to Acapulco.

One more last-ditch effort to patch up their marriage came early in 1952 when Duke went to Honolulu to film *Big Jim McLain*. After another showdown in Encino, they kissed and made up, and agreed to go to Honolulu together.

It was to be a second honeymoon, and they even had the bridal suite on the boat. It didn't work. Shortly after their arrival, Chata flew off in a huff to Encino, picked up Mama and their considerable luggage, and left for Mexico City. After depositing Mama and luggage there, she came back to the big house and called a press conference.

"Thees ees the end!" Chata announced. "I weel definitely take steps to get the divorce!" She went on to say that she was "very seeck and confused" and it was "all John's fault."

"I weel tell everything!" she declared. "I weel tell the truth!"

If she expected any action on Duke's part as a result of this public threat, she didn't get it. He went right on making movies. He'd come back from Ireland where he made *The Quiet Man* and immediately went into *Trouble Along the Way* at Warner Brothers.

As she'd been getting nowhere, Chata must have decided that she'd better go ahead with the legal steps while John was still in the country. The next thing Duke knew, Chata had gone to the leading legal counsel in Hollywood, Jerry Geisler, and was filing a suit for separate maintenance in Santa Monica.

Duke's lawyer, Frank Belcher, rushed in with a countersuit for divorce, filed in the Los Angeles Court. But he was just about a half-hour too late—which meant that Chata would get to tell her side of the story first.

When the hearings got under way, Los Angeles Superior Court looked like a theater on the night of a movie premiere, with mobs of fans besieging Duke for his autograph when he arrived on the scene. He was smiling and obliging. He pointed to the Marriage License Bureau across the street and cracked, "They've got one autograph I wish I hadn't signed!"

His good humor didn't last long. What Chata wanted was their $125,000 home and $9,350 a month support.

She had the support money all figured out:

Clothing, $746; personal effects (furs, jewelry) $499; upkeep of the estate, $1,245; household expenses, $1,983; automobile expenses, $948; gifts and entertainment, $261; travel fares, $794; telephones, $301; health and insurance, $1,518; charities, $1,023 (which charities, she didn't say)—and $650 for support of her mother!

Duke contended that, with or without her mother, she could get along very well on $900, and he was willing to throw in $1,300 for the upkeep of the estate.

He confessed that he "really didn't know" the exact state of his finances, but he produced somebody who did—his business manager, Bo Roos.

For stars in the big-money class, the business manager had become as essential as the caps on their teeth. For his percentage—usually 5 percent—he kept their tangled finances in order, advised them on investments and budgeted their incomes down to the last dime. He also saw to it that their contracts were met, and they were never short-changed.

Although studio executives hated the sight of him, Bo Roos was grudgingly respected as one of the best business managers in Hollywood. When he spoke for Duke in court, it was with authority—and he had all the figures to back him up. Regardless of his high earnings, Roos said, John Wayne was *not* a wealthy man. His money went out as soon as it came in—for taxes (he was in a high bracket), for Josephine and the children and for other essential expenses. In addition, some bad investments had eaten up a lot of his savings.

Roos testified that he had been "very concerned about Mrs. Wayne's extravagance." His pleadings with her did no good. "She just laughed and refused to take me seriously." In desperation, he had asked his wife to talk to Chata. She did, but Chata wouldn't listen to her, either.

With the financial preliminaries over, the main bout began. Chata, represented by Jerome Rosenthal of Geisler's office, threw the first punches—twenty-two of them in all, according to the bill of particulars. Duke's lawyer, Frank Belcher, had prepared his denial, plus thirty-one countercharges.

It was a shame that cameras weren't permitted in the courtroom, for as Chata got going on the stand, Duke's facial reactions were worthy of an Academy Award. They ranged from amusement (at first) to surprise, incredulity and, finally, a raging anger he could hardly control.

The inspiration for this performance was:

Chata's claim that at a party at actor John Carroll's home he had knocked her to the floor and kicked her.

He had once hit her in the Tail O' the Cock restaurant, forcing her to call the police.

At a party in the home of Mexican politician Antonio Lombardo he had dragged her by the foot the length of the living room.

He was "geeven to fits of temper," Chata said. Once, he hurled a bottle of rubbing alcohol at her. Another time, he went ranting around their home, throwing towels all over the place, because he was "deesatisfied with the number of towels in hees bathroom."

Once, she had ventured to advise him to take a role that was offered him by Republic Pictures. She got a punch in the nose for her good intentions.

In Acapulco, she had accidentally blundered into a nude swimming party her husband was enjoying with his male friends. She was very embarrassed—not at the sight, apparently, but because he bawled her out.

The high point came when Chata described the night when he came home in the wee hours and smashed the door in after the studio party. "I ask heem, wasn't eet strange that he spend the night with Gail Russell? He try to tell me eet is okay, he can do that!"

Finally, after throwing in some more tales of alleged

whacks, punches and hair-pulling inflicted by her husband when he was in his cups, she told of their last days together, on that "second honeymoon" in Honolulu.

She was angered when he went off with his friends to a stag party at Waikiki Beach. She was more angered when he came home, very late, with a bite on his neck.

"What kind of bite?" Judge Allen Ashburn wanted to know.

Chata lowered her eyes demurely. "Eet was a human being bite," she said.

She had weathered that shock, but the last straw was the time he had become drunk and abusive at a party and threw her shawl in a mud puddle. That wasn't all. Most of the night, he had pounded on the wall of their adjoining bedroom, calling her vile names, and the next morning he told her he was "sick and tired of me, and he threw pillows at me."

"What kind of names did he call you?" Judge Ashburn asked.

As Chata looked properly flustered, her lawyer stepped into the breach, pointing out that they weren't fit for a lady to repeat.

"All right," Judge Ashburn agreed, "just whisper them to me." Chata did—while titters broke out in the courtroom, and the judge had to wield his gavel to restore order.

Even Duke had to smile when, after tearing him to shreds, Chata wound up by saying, "The demon rum ees to blame for hees hehavior. He have heart of gold when he ees sober."

Thoroughly titillated by all these spicy revelations, the courtroom spectators got more when Attorney Rosenthal made an emotional summation, to the effect that Chata had "learned the horror of the bottle under the guidance, tutelage, and even under the roof of Mr. Wayne." She had been enticed to "live under the same roof with John Wayne for two years while he was still married, though estranged, from his first wife. . . ."

Of course, most of these juicy tidbits reached the newspapers the next day. Naturally, too, the headlines and photos played up the testimony linking Duke and Gail Russell.

Now, he was mad enough to let Chata have it with both barrels, and he came up with plenty of ammunition:

In June 1950, Chata and her mother became drunk in Mexico City. Her mother hit Chata, and she blamed her bruised face on her husband—who, at the time, was making a movie in Moab, Utah.

In August 1950, during a dinner party for the troup of a film he was making in Mexico, Chata became drunk and fell downstairs, striking her head. Again, she accused him of injuring her.

In November 1950, she refused to leave a party and fell on the floor. When he tried to pick her up she kicked at him but missed, hitting someone else.

In December 1951, she refused to leave a nightclub. She sent for her bathing suit, went swimming, came back and slept among the tables.

In January 1952, she claimed she was "ill, nervous and exhausted" and what she needed was a trip to Las Vegas. Instead of relaxing, she spent the time drinking and gambling away "a large sum of money."

In April or May of 1952, she refused to leave a party in Honolulu and appeared at breakfast the next morning "bruised, intoxicated, her clothing disheveled and appearing to have numerous grass stains."

From June to July 1952, the bill of particulars went on, Mrs. Wayne toured Mexico City nightclubs with "men other than her husband" and footed the bills. She was escorted to the plane by a man who gave her an orchid—and a fond embrace.

As a clincher, Duke's lawyer introduced some of Chata's doodles Duke had discovered, linking her name with Nicky Hilton's. He had also discovered that Nicky spent a week at their home while he was in Hawaii. Nicky, divorced from Liz Taylor, had taken up with Betsy von Furstenberg, who was a friend of Chata's. The three of them staunchly declared that poor Nicky had been in an auto accident and had had no place to stay while he recovered. Considering that Nicky's father owned all those great hotels in Los Angeles and elsewhere, not to mention a few mansions here and there, this was pretty hard to believe.

Nicky was subpoenaed, but he never got a chance to testify. Though he protested his innocence strongly, maybe it was just as well.

At that point, everybody concerned was ready to call the battle of the bottles to a halt and make some kind of sensible agreement. Everybody except Duke, that is.

To anybody who'd listen, he made clear exactly how he felt. "Nobody's going to call me a yellow-bellied coward, backing down and going behind closed doors to settle this thing. What would the people who go to see my movies think if I did a thing like that? No, I want to go through with it right out in the open, no matter what she does!"

His friends—and that included just about everyone in Hollywood who knew him—were worried. There were ugly rumors going around. It was whispered that

Chata intended to accuse Duke of being sterile, impotent, and worse!

Duke wasn't aware of this, but among many who were was writer Lloyd Shearer who came to interview him.

As Duke went into his usual harangue about how the people would despise him if he did such a cowardly thing as going behind closed doors, Shearer interrupted. "Wait a minute, Duke," he said. "Aren't you exaggerating this because you're so close to it? When the people across the country who see your films get out of bed tomorrow, they're not going to be asking, 'What will John Wayne do today?' They'll be asking, 'What time is it?'"

Duke threw back his head and roared. "You son-of-a-bitch!" he shouted, giving Shearer the bone-crushing clap on the shoulder with which he denotes affection and/or approval.

To this day, Shearer doesn't know whether his talk with Duke had anything to do with it—but the next day, the public mud-slinging ended and a settlement was reached.

Judge Ashburn called it a draw, granting a divorce to both parties.

Chata got much less than she bargained for—$1,100 a month for ten years, plus fees connected with the case amounting to $12,500. Duke agreed to allow her to live on the estate and to pay for the upkeep until the divorce became final a year later. But he kept the estate. And he didn't have to support Chata's mother. If Chata had won that point, it could have set a precedent that would have upset California courts for years to come.

There was a strange, sad ending to the love story of Duke and Chata.

After the divorce became final, Chata talked to Hollywood writer Vernon Scott before returning to Mexico City. The fire, the flashing smile were gone. She was spent and drawn, and very subdued.

"I wanted to have a good life, a good home with my husband. That was all I wanted—to be a good wife, and make heem happy. But eet was not to be. Now, eet ees all gone. My career—that ees gone, too. I feel so lost, so confused. . . ."

Many months later, a small item appeared in the papers. The U.S. government had claimed $41,901 in taxes from John Wayne because his ex-wife had returned to Mexico City and was therefore an alien, not subject to deductions.

The case was decided in Wayne's favor because nobody could possibly know whether Chata intended to remain in Mexico City as an alien or not.

Shortly after her return there, Chata reportedly suffered a heart attack. At age thirty-six, she was dead.

Chapter 9

GAIL—THE WOMAN HE TRIED TO SAVE

"Why did Chata have to drag that poor kid's name into this? I never had anything to do with Miss Russell except to make a couple of pictures with her!"

———◆—◆◆◆—◆———

Gail Russell wasn't like other Hollywood actresses. That seemed to be her trouble, from the beginning.

At Santa Monica High School she was a loner, a girl who didn't seem to want friends and who was happiest with her painting and drawing. She could do everything from caricatures to fashion sketches, and her work was beautiful.

Withdrawn as she was, her own beauty was bound to attract attention. In a community where talent scouts were always on the lookout for lovely young things, word quickly reached them about the stunning brunette at Santa Monica High. She was tall and slender, with long, dark hair curling naturally around a finely chiseled face. Her eyes were large, luminous and gray-green. By the time she was seventeen a scout had signed her to a contract.

Gail's mother was thrilled. They'd had a difficult life, very insecure, with many moves and hardships and to her it seemed like an answer to prayer. Now her daughter would have the best of everything.

Gail was simply terrified. Going through the usual grooming process at the studio, with drama and diction lessons and analysis of everything from her makeup to the way she walked, Gail died a thousand deaths. Other girls reveled in it, but not Gail.

Grimly, she did as she was told. She didn't want to let her mother down, and she was too painfully shy to confide her fears to anyone.

She made her debut in a small part in a Henry Aldrich film. Perhaps she was able to forget her shyness when she was actually in front of the cameras, pretending to be someone else. Whatever it was, she came through as that rare find, a beauty who could act.

Studio heads were quick to appreciate it and immediately saw a goldmine in Gail. Her second role was a starring part opposite Ray Milland in *The Uninvited*.

The reviews she got were raves. One even described her as a "near genius."

Instead of giving her confidence, this frightened her even more. She was only nineteen, with no experience, and had been pushed into top roles much too fast to be sure of herself.

She was having a rough time, too, with the Hollywood wolf pack. Along with her other troubles, Gail had to try to cope with older, jaded actors and producers on the make. She didn't know how to handle them, and it was a constant source of misery.

One day, seeing her in tears, a kindly technician handed her a paper cup. "Here, drink this," he said. "It'll make you feel better."

She gulped it down. The raw whiskey burned her throat, but it gave her a warm feeling and calmed her screaming nerves. Liquor, she knew, was strictly forbidden on the set, but she used some mouthwash and went back to work. Nobody noticed.

The pressure increased when she was given a choice starring role in *Our Hearts Were Young and Gay*. By this time, she was sneaking out to a little bar across from the studio whenever she got the chance.

As her career gained momentum, so did her drinking. She learned that there was always somebody around who would bring liquor onto the set, for a price.

There were rumors about Gail's drinking, but she was able to stay at the top. She was only in her early twenties when she was cast opposite John Wayne in *Angel and the Badman*, in 1946.

He wasn't like any of the other actors she'd known. He was kind and considerate, and when he smiled it was like the sun coming out. He was so big and strong, too, the kind of person you could lean on. He was exactly the kind of man Gail needed, and if she fell madly in love with him, it was understandable.

Duke was having his troubles with Chata, and if he found shy, lovely Gail appealing, that was understandable, too. With her complete lack of pretention and ambition, she was a refreshing change from most of the actresses he knew.

He soon sensed her great loneliness and insecurity and went out of his way to be friendly. In interviews, he never failed to bring up her name, praising her to the skies.

Gail had never been so happy. She felt cherished and protected as she never had been before. There were rumors about Duke's problems with Chata, and if Gail dreamed a few dreams about someday becoming Mrs. Wayne, who could blame her?

Duke might have had a few dreams, too. Certainly, he was unhappy at home, though he was still trying to make a go of it with Chata. Still, though he might not admit it to himself, he couldn't help but be attracted to beautiful, quiet Gail, who was the complete opposite of Chata.

They were drawn together by a mutual need, and as they began to spend more time together away from the cameras, during breaks or at lunch, the usual Hollywood "hot romance" rumors started.

"That's a lot of bullshit!" Duke would bellow to anyone who dared mention it to him. "Miss Russell and I are working together on a picture, we're friends, and that's it."

Gail was more upset. To her, the rumors were not only a threat to her career, but to the relationship with

Duke that she was desperately clinging to as the only solid rock in the stormy sea of her world. The only thing that seemed to steady her was another drink. . . .

Today, the phony moral facade has been stripped away from Hollywood. The sexual capers of the stars are all right out in the open—mate-switching, living together and having babies out of wedlock—and nobody thinks anything of it.

Of course, the same things were going on in 1946. The only difference was that they were carefully hidden from the public, and stars were carefully pictured as pillars of virtue, lest a hint of scandal would cause public disapproval and, most important, a loss of money at the box office.

Today, the story of Duke and Gail and Chata might have turned out quite differently. But it was 1946, and they were bound by the unrealistic moral standards of the time.

When gossip got around that Duke had given Gail a car, an incident that wouldn't cause a ripple today, it was a major crisis, with Chata screaming and making the most of her position as the wronged wife—another moral rule of the time.

Shrewdly, Chata knew it gave her a certain advantage. It was a veiled threat of exposure that, in the narrow-minded forties, she could damage Duke's career.

Apparently, she had one thing in common with Josie—she didn't really know the man she married.

Duke was not only smart enough to see right through her maneuvers, but also intelligent enough to realize

86

that he had reached a status in the business where such "scandals" really couldn't hurt him very much.

What did hurt him was that all the gossip and accusations were so unfair. He hadn't given Gail a car, but merely loaned her a down payment when her old car broke down and she needed one to get to the studio.

He was hurt because of what the rumors could do to Gail, not himself. He was strong enough to shrug or laugh off such things. But he knew she wasn't, and he knew how terribly hard it was for her.

Gail had found a way to kill the pain. All it took was a couple of drinks. . . .

The night of the party celebrating the end of the picture was the happiest Gail had ever known.

She didn't retreat to a corner as she usually did at such affairs. Duke wouldn't let her.

When she got there, the party was already in full swing, and Duke, with his size and warmth, dominated it all. She was about to sit down at a table where she'd be unnoticed when he spied her.

"Hey, here's our star!" he called and, in a few strides, came over, took her by the hand and led her right into the center of the crowd. "Now, will somebody fix a very special drink for our star?"

The drink and Duke's smile gave her a glow, and she found herself really enjoying these people she hardly knew, though she worked with them every day—the technicians, the cameramen, the script girls—everybody who had anything to do with making the picture. Along with Duke, she talked and laughed with them and had a wonderful time.

The party went on and on, long past midnight, and

everybody was getting pretty high. "C'mon," Duke said to Gail. "I think I'd better take you home."

She was happy to go—with him. She was happy to be anywhere with him.

When they got to her house, her mother was still up, and she invited him in for a nightcap. Duke accepted readily. He wasn't eager to go home and face Chata. They had a pleasant time and more than one nightcap, and he began to feel the effects. He called a cab to take him home.

Gail never knew about the terrible scene with Chata when he got home, or that Chata was so jealous of her that she stormed back to Mexico City when she learned that they were to be teamed again in *Wake of the Red Witch*.

Duke never told her anything about that. On the set, he was as kind, gentle and friendly as before, but it wasn't the same. Often, he seemed preoccupied with his own thoughts, thoughts he didn't share with her.

They got through the picture, and there was a party, but it wasn't any fun. Not for Gail. Or Duke.

She was left with her broken dreams. "He never really cared about me," she thought. "He was just being kind, out of pity. . . ."

She didn't know that Duke was doing his best to protect her because he knew how vulnerable she was. For her sake, he couldn't risk the slightest involvement. And along with other considerations, that meant he couldn't see her anymore—or at least until he got things squared away with Chata.

Wake of the Red Witch was released in 1949. That same year, Gail Russell married Guy Madison.

He was a big, handsome young actor with a very promising career. And to many people he had all the qualities of a young John Wayne. He even looked like him, with wavy brown hair and strong features. He came from a good family and, unlike the usual Hollywood types, he was forthright and sincere.

For a while it looked as if Gail had found real happiness at last. Feverishly, she tried to capture it.

At the time they married, Gail's career was at its peak. Guys was in the doldrums. Like Gail, he had been an overnight success. A clever agent, Helen Ainsworth, had seen his picture in a Navy magazine, and before Guy quite knew what was happening to him, he was cast in a brief part in a Selznick picture, *Since You Went Away*, done while he was on Navy leave. The fan clamor for him was so strong that Selznick immediately gave him a contract, effective when he got out of the Navy.

Like Gail, he learned that it takes a lot more than good looks and a stroke of good fortune to become a movie star. Utterly without training or experience, Guy simply could not act. Within a short time, Selznick dropped him.

Sensible and methodical—two of his qualities that Gail found comforting, because she lacked them—Guy faced his problem the right way. He took what parts he could get and studied to improve. Eventually, his efforts paid off handsomely when he became TV's *Wild Bill Hickok*.

But when he married Gail, that success was several years away. There they were, two green youngsters floundering in the backwash of a tidal wave of success that had hit them too fast, too soon.

At first, Gail tried to hide her drinking from Guy, but it didn't take him long to realize that the brown liquid in her cup wasn't coffee. Already she'd reached the point where it took a few slugs of whiskey in the morning to go to work or face an interview—or anything at all.

Guy wasn't angry. He understood her fears and tried to help. He sent her to a doctor who put her on a strict diet. Liquor and cigarettes were out. She was to drink a gallon of water a day and be in bed at nine. When she was at home, Guy helped her to stay with her routine. When she was at work, there was still the familiar studio bootlegger to lure her off it.

Their first separation came thirteen months after they were married. It took them only ten days to find out how much they wanted and needed each other, and Gail rushed back into Guy's outstretched arms.

With a couple of good parts, his career was picking up. Gail's was hitting the skids. More and more production delays due to her "illness" made producers reluctant to hire her.

A long stay in a sanatorium didn't do any good. She tried joining Alcoholics Anonymous, but failed to find the help it gave to so many others, probably because she was too shy to talk about her problems.

In 1953, Gail and Guy separated again, this time for a much longer time. It was then that Gail was arrested for drunken driving. She was fined $50 and placed on two years' probation.

She and Guy were reconciled for a brief time, but early in 1954 Gail sued for divorce, charging "extreme cruelty," and was awarded a generous alimony, depending on Guy's income.

With her career and her marriage in ruins, Gail

became distrustful of even good friends who tried to help her, and again turned to the bottle for solace. She was arrested again for drunken driving, this time fined $450, which she didn't have. It was Guy Madison who came to her aid. He parked on a side street to avoid more headlines for her, slipped into the building and paid her fine.

Gail went back to the doctors and the sanatorium in another effort to pull herself together. She had just come back when Chata Wayne tore her apart.

Chata's charge that he had "spent the night" with Gail after the party at the end of *Angel and the Badman* was the one thing in the whole mess that made Duke boiling mad. Whatever Chata threw at him he could take, but he couldn't take seeing Gail, who was completely innocent of any wrongdoing, made the object of mud-slinging. He was one of the few people who knew Gail and her weakness well enough to realize what a devastating effect it could have on her.

No matter what his lawyers thought, he told the press exactly what he thought. "That poor kid! Why did her name have to be dragged into this? We worked in a couple of pictures together, we were friends, and I stopped in at her house that night. Her mother was there, and we all had a couple of drinks. That's all there was to it. I deeply regret that Miss Russell has been subjected to this kind of mud-slinging. Maybe I'd better start doing some mud-slinging of my own!"

It was at that point that the Wayne divorce case became a free-for-all, until cooler heads prevailed and put a stop to it.

Gail had managed to go to court to corroborate Duke's testimony of her innocence, and Duke managed to have a word with her. She seemed to be in a daze. "Listen to me, Gail," he said. "Please! I want you to remember this. If there's ever anything I can do for you, *anything* at all, I want you to call on me. Now, will you promise to do that?"

She nodded, unable to speak, and walked away. What could he do for her? Already there were rumors about his interest in a Peruvian beauty named Pilar Palette. Besides, what could he do *now*, that wouldn't make matters worse?

Her worst binge followed the trial. This time, she wasn't asked to go into a sanatorium. She was rushed there, to save her life, and didn't come out for a year.

When she did, she came back to the same misery. Heartless producers asked her bluntly, "Are you still an alcoholic?" When she told them she wasn't, they wouldn't hire her anyway. A worse blow was Guy's remarriage to Sheila Connolly and the news that they were expecting a baby. She'd lost him for good, now.

Her third arrest for drunken driving followed. This time, it was really bad. In addition to a $1,000 fine and losing her license, she had smashed into a cafe and faced a suit for injuries filed by one of the employees.

"I don't know how many drinks I had," she told police. "Maybe two, maybe four. Oh, I don't know, and it isn't anybody's business!" She covered her face with her hands and sobbed.

Again it was Guy who quietly arrived to pay the fines. Again, Gail went off to the sanatorium.

The story was splashed in headlines all over the country, with pictures of Gail, distraught and disheveled, but still beautiful. Of course, it was seen by John Wayne.

"Why didn't she call me?" he thought. "*Why*? Maybe I could have helped. I still feel so damn bad about what happened to her at that trial. Well, this time I'm going to try to help her, whether she calls me or not."

When Gail came back this time, she didn't have to go through the dreaded humiliation of going the rounds and facing producers who only knew that she was a lush and didn't want her. There was a job waiting for her. And not just a minor role, but a starring part, opposite Randolph Scott in *Seven Men From Now*.

The picture was produced by Batjac—which was John Wayne's company.

"Aren't you taking a big chance?" a close friend asked Duke. "If that girl doesn't make it through the shooting, if she goes off the deep end again and has to quit, it will cost you a fortune."

Duke nodded. "I know that," he said, "but I don't think it will happen. It's about time somebody gives her a chance to get back on her feet. She's still beautiful, and she always was a fine actress. She'll come through. Anyway, I feel it's the least I can do after that beating she took from Chata."

Gail knew she had more than a job. She had a friend—one person in her troubled world who really wanted to help. And Duke was right—she didn't let him down. She joined AA again. She joined a church. On location in Big Bear, California, she went along with the others to relax at a local bar after the day's work, but she drank only ginger ale.

The picture was finished on time and, even if it wasn't outstanding, it was a good, solid Western that brought money into the box office.

As a result, Gail got some other offers, mostly for TV shows, and for a while it looked as if she was really on the way back. And nobody was happier about that than John Wayne.

At this time, of course, he was happily married to Pilar. Gail wasn't happily married to anybody. And she was finding, once again, that success can't cure the ache of loneliness. She went back to the only cure she knew.

It didn't take long for word to get around that she was off the wagon and, again, parts became nonexistent.

Her alimony payments from Guy were enough to provide her with a comfortable, though modest living. Early in 1961, she moved into a $130 a month apartment on Bentley Avenue in Los Angeles, calling herself "Mrs. Moseley" in an attempt to avoid recognition (Guy's real name was Robert Moseley). The neighbors saw her in the backyard painting pictures. She was good at it and seemed to be taking her work seriously. They'd see her riding her bicycle or hitting golf balls to keep in shape. They tried to be friendly, but she was merely polite in return and clearly didn't want their friendship.

Late in August, they noticed that her lights were burning all night, two nights in a row. They called the police.

She was lying on the living room floor, an empty vodka bottle near her hand. There were more empty bottles strewn throughout the apartment, along with a lot of paintings indicating a pathetic try to start another career. The girl who in 1947 was hailed as "Star of Tomorrow" was pronounced dead on August 28, 1961, at the age of thirty-six, due to "natural causes."

Is loneliness a natural cause? Is despair?

"Nobody ever came to see her," a neighbor said, "except the man from AA, once a month."

Even the firm, lasting friendship of John Wayne had failed to save her. Maybe because she didn't want to be saved.

Chapter 10

PILAR—A NEW KIND OF LUST

"I can tell you why I love her. I have a lust for her dignity. I look at her wonderfully classic face, and I see hidden in it a sense of humor that I love. I think of wonderful, exciting, decent things when I look at her. . . ."

———◄••►———

It was after he'd finished *Big Jim McLain* on that wild location trip to Hawaii that Duke decided to get away from it all. Actually, with Chata holed up in their Encino mansion delivering pronouncements about the " 'orrible theengs that 'appened in 'Onolulu" and announcing her intentions of seeking a divorce, he didn't have much choice.

He chose to go to Peru, to take a look at the film-making there and other investment possibilities. If the trip wasn't profitable, at least it would put a lot of distance between him and Chata. He'd met a young sportsman named Dick Weldy, who among other ventures represented Panagra Airlines, and Dick was happy to arrange the trip for Duke. Having a famous movie star like John Wayne visit Peru—via Panagra, of course—was great publicity.

Duke liked Weldy because they had a lot in common. Both were the big, strong outdoor type who weren't afraid of encounters with dangerous animals and were handy with a gun. One of Weldy's favorite occupations was capturing animals—from man-eating tigers to deadly pythons—and selling or renting them to circuses and movie companies.

The two men wound up in a small Peruvian village called Tingo Maria, where some of the film-making Duke wanted to see was in progress.

Exactly what happened in Tingo Maria depends on whose version you want to believe. *Confidential* magazine, at that time so notorious (and popular) that movie studios blacklisted any writer caught working for it, came out with a sizzling story.

According to *Confidential*, the red carpet had been rolled out upon the arrival of the famous John Wayne, and that included supplying him with an assortment of available (in every sense of the word) local beauties. But the gals found Big John a big bore and turned him down after one date, according to the story.

Still pining for feminine companionship (the story

went on), he stole his "best friend's" wife. The accompanying photos, captioned "Going . . . Going . . . Gone!" showed one picture with Weldy sitting between Duke and a raven-haired beauty, the next picture with the raven-haired beauty sitting between Duke and Weldy, and finally, a picture with Duke and the raven-haired beauty smiling straight at the cameras, cozily cheek-to-cheek!

The lady, it turned out, was a Peruvian actress, Pilar Palette—who also happened to be Mrs. Weldy.

Obviously, there were some things very wrong with the story. In the first place, Dick Weldy couldn't be described as Duke's "best friend" when they'd hardly become acquainted. And the snide slurs about the Wayne prowess with the local gals were the kind of baseless innuendos *Confidential* managed to get away with (for one big reason—under the laws of libel, the injured party must prove that the alleged libel affected his ability to make a living. Few stars were able to do that—certainly not John Wayne who had moved up to the Top Ten on the box-office lists!).

It didn't stand to reason, either, that the trio would allow themselves to be photographed in a compromising situation without their consent. But there they were, completely relaxed and happily smiling for the birdie.

Undoubtedly, they were all convinced that the innocent (they thought) photos showing them having a good time in Peru would help to attract tourists and businessmen to the area.

Much later, Pilar said that all she remembered about the evening was Duke's impressive size and that when he shook hands with her, it was "like being hit with a telephone pole!"

When the nasty *Confidential* story came out, Duke had his hands full trying to cope with the sensational divorce from Chata. Anyway, like many another star, he had learned that bad publicity was best ignored. A fight would only attract attention and increase the sale of the magazine.

Big game hunter Dick Weldy didn't see it that way. He was accused of going after publisher Robert Harrison with a gun. Somehow, the whole thing was smoothed over and labeled a mistake, and that was the end of it.

But for Duke and Pilar, it was the beginning.

Duke had come back from making *The Quiet Man* in Ireland in the fall of 1952 and reported to Warner Brothers for *Trouble Along the Way*. By an amazing coincidence, who should he run into in the Green Room but Pilar!

Unlike Chata, whose English was far from perfect, Pilar had spent much time in the United States, spoke English beautifully, and had many friends in Hollywood, which explains her presence at lunch in the studio commissary.

All the reports, before and since, that pictured Pilar as a "leading Peruvian actress" were scoffed at by Duke himself in his usual forthright manner. "She did appear in a couple of pictures," he said, "because she was there and they needed someone with long, black hair. That was all there was to it. She never had a serious, full-time acting career." Considering what Duke was going through with Chata, he'd hardly be attracted to another career actress.

In what Pilar described later as a "hands across the

Panama Canal" gesture, Duke asked her out to dinner.

"I've had dinner with him almost every night since that day," she laughs.

It wasn't love at first sight. Pilar was having her own marital troubles. She and Weldy had parted, and divorce was inevitable. It was only natural that she and Duke would find solace in each other's company.

Gradually, they found that they were miserable when they were apart. "Duke never really proposed to me," Pilar says with a smile. "We just had a kind of understanding between us that we would be married when we were legally free."

The closest he came to proposing was showing her the big white house he still owned, vacant since Chata's departure.

"We could sell it and get another house, if you feel you can't be happy here," he said.

She threw her arms around him and kissed him. "I can be happy anywhere with you!"

That settled it. They still had to wait awhile, but in the meantime, because their romance was being widely covered in the press, Duke thought it best to make a formal announcement.

"Pilar has brought me a great deal of happiness," he said. "I believe in companionship and I have to admit I like to be married. To the right girl, of course."

Under California law, Duke's divorce wouldn't become final for a year. In the fall of 1954, the time was almost up, and when he went back to Hawaii to make *The Sea Chase*, Pilar went along, too.

If Pilar had any qualms about Duke's teaming in the picture with the glamorous Lana Turner, they were soon quieted. From the outset, Duke and La Turner didn't hit it off at all, and reports of their feuding on the set grew more and more frequent.

Off the set, everything was idyllic as Duke and Pilar spent happy hours planning their future together. At last, in October, the word they'd been waiting for came—first for Pilar, who learned that her marriage to Dick Weldy had been annulled. A few days later, Duke got a call from his lawyer, Frank Belcher, telling him the divorce had been finalized and he was free to marry.

They wasted no time. That very evening, on November 1, 1954, Duke and Pilar were married by a Hawaiian justice of the peace.

In spite of the short notice, it turned out to be the most beautiful wedding any couple could wish. The *Sea Chase* cast had been invited to stay at Territorial Senator William H. Hill's fabulous mansion, once the home of a Hawaiian king, and the ceremony was held in the beautiful gardens. All the Hawaiian people in the town of Kailua closed their shops, put on their best clothes and came. The whole cast and crew of the picture were there (with the notable exception of Miss Turner, who had left for the States in a huff as soon as her work was finished).

Pilar was a vision in a pink organdy cocktail dress. Director John Farrow gave the bride away, and a good friend of Duke's, wealthy sportsman Francis H. I. Brown of Pebble Beach, was best man.

As they were pronounced man and wife, the sun sank into the Pacific in the most gorgeous sunset they had ever seen. "It was the most romantic place in the whole world," Pilar remembers.

After the wedding the Hawaiians lit torches, and there was singing and dancing and feasting until it was time for Duke and Pilar to go to the airport, where they were decked with flowers in a grand aloha as they left for Honolulu and the bridal suite of the Royal Hawaiian Hotel.

Cornered by the press the next day, they were happy to kiss for the cameras. "This is the greatest thing that ever happened to me," Duke announced. "I've had lots of wonderful things happen, but this is the best."

Most people want to honeymoon in Hawaii. Duke and Pilar reversed that—they were eager to get back to California, to their own home.

"We've been traveling all over the world," Duke explained to reporters, "and we'll be happy just to sit by the hearth for a while."

Inevitably, he was asked about his preference for Latin girls—a question he was getting tired of but still tried to answer civilly.

"I just like them," he said flatly, "the way some men like blondes. To me, they seem more warm, and direct, and down-to-earth. But each of my wives has been entirely different.

"I don't have anything against American women," he went on, loyally. "In fact, the women I married were all as much American as Latin. My first wife was brought up in Texas. Esperanza had spent a lot of time in this country, in Florida and elsewhere, before I met her. And Pilar has been here a great deal and speaks English perfectly."

No, he stated emphatically, Pilar didn't want a career. Her work in films had never amounted to more than a little fun fling anyway.

When Duke went back to work after his "at home" honeymoon, he wisely refused to fall into the pattern of separating his wife from his work that had widened his estrangement from Josie. Whenever possible, Pilar went with him on location and visited him on the set. Once, when she was asked whether she ever became jealous when he played those hot love scenes with his leading ladies, she laughed. "Oh, no! I'm usually right there, watching. And afterward, I'll tell him how good I thought it was!"

Duke's co-workers quickly accepted Pilar, whom they regarded as a "real lady" as well as a good sport who never complained about location hardships or interfered with their work. And like Duke, they appreciated her pixie sense of humor.

Once, Duke was asked whether his wife had any faults. He thought for a moment, then grinned. "Yes," he said. "her love of sneaky practical jokes and black and white clothes! I shop and get her colored things, and she pretends to like them and will even wear them a few times, but then goes back to black and white!"

"The nicest thing that happened since our marriage," as Pilar put it, occurred on March 31, 1956, when their first child, Aissa Maria, was born—even if it was pretty hectic.

While telling Pilar, over and over, "Now, don't get nervous," as he drove her to St. Joseph's Hospital, Duke took a wrong turn.

"He was so upset," laughs Pilar, "because he'd lived in the Valley half his life and knew all the roads. Luckily, the baby was eleven hours late."

When Duke was ushered in to see his new daughter, Pilar expected some tender words she would cherish for years.

"Move over! I'm pooped!" Duke mumbled, and

flopped on the bed beside her, completely exhausted.

Game as she was, Pilar was finding those location trips with Duke rough going. She could count on her mother (who was staying with the Waynes for a while) to take good care of little Aissa.

What she didn't count on were the very rough conditions cast and crew often endured on these jaunts. She found out just how rough they could be when she flew to Gadames, in the Sahara Desert, in response to Duke's cable, "It is beautiful here. Miss you. Please join me right away."

After a long, weary flight with many changes, Pilar arrived at Gadames with four large cans of hot dogs for her beloved. (No, she didn't forget the mustard.)

Gadames was an oasis where *The Legend of the Lost*, co-starring Sophia Loren and Rossano Brazzi, was being produced by Duke's company, Batjac. Gadames was beautiful, all right, but there was only one large house for the cast, with no phones or electricity, and there was nothing to do at night but crawl under the blankets and shiver when the temperature dropped to twenty below zero.

Pilar marveled at stoic Sophia, who had to do a scene in icy water four times and went through it without a whimper. As for Pilar, she'd had it.

When Duke went to Tokyo to make *The Barbarian and the Geisha*, she decided to stay at home.

She was alone in the big house with little Aissa, except for two maids who lived in a wing downstairs, and she had moved the baby's crib into her own room to be close to her in case she should cry during the night, even though, at twenty-two months, Aissa slept soundly through the night.

At three o'clock in the morning, on January 14, 1958, Pilar who also slept soundly, was awakened by sharp barking. Still half asleep, she wondered, ''What in the world can be wrong with Blackie?'' The family pet, a little black dachshund, never barked without a reason.

Then it hit her. The acrid smell of smoke and a strange glow in the room. Leaping out of bed, she saw flames licking at the edge of the carpet!

Grabbing Aissa from her crib, she rushed downstairs to arouse the maids, Consuelo and Angelica Saldana, and one of their children who was staying there.

''Call the fire department!'' she shouted to Consuelo. Handing Aissa to Angelica, she told her to get the children out of the house—fast.

There was a fire extinguisher downstairs; she grabbed it and rushed back upstairs. As she got to the top of the stairs, the flames suddenly burst across the carpet, hitting the record player and the records that exploded like fireworks on the Fourth of July. Trying not to inhale the smoke, she managed to grope her way downstairs, to find the maids, children and three dogs huddled there. Terrified for her safety, the maids had refused to leave.

Outside, as fire engines arrived with sirens screaming, the first person to come on the scene was Robert Morrison, Duke's brother. Duke and his ''little brother'' had remained close all through the years, and Bob lived close by. Though he never became an actor, he was doing well behind the cameras, directing and producing.

There was no sign of Pilar and the others and Bob was frantic. Flames were shooting skyward from the second story. Firemen had to keep Bob from rushing into the house. On the lawn, Duke's daughter, Toni, who had married and also lived close by, and Mrs. Web Overlander, wife of Duke's makeup man of many years, stood crying helplessly.

Then through the smoke, Bob saw something moving near the kitchen door. "There they are!" he shouted, sprinting toward them as fast as he could.

It wasn't until he got them all—Pilar and Aissa, the maids and a little boy, and three dogs—safely settled in Toni's house that Mrs. Overlander noticed a nasty burn on Pilar's arm. Pilar had been in such a state of shock that she hadn't even felt it.

Firemen fought the blaze for over an hour. When it was finally extinguished, the entire second story was a smoldering ruin, the rest of the house badly damaged by smoke and water. Many valuable antiques and personal belongings had been destroyed, and the whole damage was estimated at $500,000. The house could be rebuilt, but it would take months.

The whole family—including Duke, who was on the phone constantly from the time the news reached him—was simply tremendously grateful that no one had been hurt. And they were tickled when all the newspapers featured a picture of little Blackie, the hero of the hour, who would henceforth lead a very spoiled dog's life.

Another cause for gratitude could be shared by cinema historians everywhere. In the midst of the holocaust, one thoughtful fireman had carefully removed from a downstairs den all the irreplaceable mementos of John Wayne's career.

Maybe it was the strain of the whole experience—

having to live in temporary quarters, replacing their belongings, taking care of the hundred-and-one details of the renovation—but by the time the Waynes were ready to move back into their home in September, they were also ready to announce the end of their marriage.

Pilar voiced an old, familiar complaint. "Unfortunately, business is sometimes more important to a man than his wife. How can a wife live with a man who, in four years of marriage, spends two-and-a-half on location? And when he does come home, he spends all of his time on business affairs."

Duke's comment was, "Pilar and I can't seem to get any warmth and understanding into our marriage anymore. It's been coming for some time. I suppose it will end in divorce."

The day after they made this public announcement, they kissed and made up and called the whole thing off.

"It was hot, and we were moving, and—well, I'm Latin, you know, and I sometimes explode," Pilar explained, apologetically.

"I guess I am wrapped up in my business affairs too much," Duke admitted sheepishly, "and when I'm making a movie, I am away for three or four months at a time."

Then he grinned broadly. "It looked like we were going to separate, but everything's okay now. We had a tiff, but we reconciled, and I'm glad."

Both had recognized the dangers before it was too late and at the time were willing to compromise. Once more, Pilar went to visit Duke on location, and if the place was full of bugs and the plumbing was nonexistent—so what? On his part, Duke tried to be a more attentive husband when he was home, cutting down on business sessions and poker parties with his pals.

Together, they shared sorrow when Pilar's second pregnancy ended in miscarriage at five months, a tragedy that affected her deeply because she was afraid she could never have another baby.

When she became pregnant again in 1961, her doctor had to reassure her that it was perfectly all right for her and Aissa to join Duke in Africa, where he was making *Hatari*, provided they didn't stay too long.

The doctor was right. On Washington's Birthday, 1962, Duke got back from Paris just in time to welcome an eight-pound, two-ounce boy they named John Ethan Wayne.

Four years later, on exactly the same day and in the same place—St. Joseph's Hospital—a tiny charmer named Marisa was born.

By that time, their children had acquired a number of nieces and nephews—grandchildren of Duke's marriage to Josie—some of them older than they were. But they all managed to mix together beautifully.

"I sometimes have the feeling," Pilar confessed once, thoughtfully, "that it was really a shame that Duke and Josephine didn't stay together, because they've both done such a wonderful job in raising their children.

"But then," she added with a wistful little smile, "what would have become of me? I couldn't live without him."

In the summer of 1973, a Hollywood columnist began to circulate persistent rumors that John Wayne's third marriage was in trouble. Immediately, the gossip began to fly.

Early in 1974, divorce plans were finally announced. Pilar confessed, "The reason for our fights was stubbornness. There was never any compromise." She added, "I still love him."

After twenty years of marriage, they moved into separate houses, both in Newport Beach, California. Duke called every day. When Pilar talked about their differences, she sounded much as Josie had in 1944. Duke was a wonderful father. But he couldn't stay home and be quietly domestic, even when he wasn't working on a picture. She admitted sadly that this restless energy was an important part of the Duke but concluded that they were just too different. They got on each other's nerves.

For several years now, they have lived mostly apart, meeting occasionally for dinner and talking daily by phone. But their attempts to reconcile—they tried in 1974 and 1977—have not succeeded.

Chapter 11

SEVEN IS A LUCKY NUMBER

"We've been very lucky with our kids. They've never given us cause to get really angry. I love my children—love all kids, as a matter of fact—and they're sensitive enough to realize it. So if they do something I don't like, I really don't have to do much to them except show disappointment. . . ."

In Hollywood, where stars' children are prone to wind up with giant-size neuroses whether their parents split up or not, John Wayne's brood is regarded as a real phenomenon. None of them has ever been in trouble with the law, arrested for drunk driving or on drug charges, or even for running away from home or school. Anyone who has met any of them knows that they are well behaved, well spoken, friendly and outgoing, and utterly without pretentions. In a place where the phrase "I want my children to lead normal lives" is an old and meaningless cliché, John Wayne is one of the very few stars who has succeeded in doing just that—even if many other stars would consider his methods unusual, to say the least.

When his children were babies, he spoiled them terribly. He'd rush home, arms loaded with expensive toys for them, even though they already had enough to stock Macy's at Christmas. He'd pick them up and cuddle them at the slightest whimper, and get down on the floor and play with them, and talk baby talk to them. That's right. There was Duke, the big, hard-bitten hero of many a battle, onscreen and off, talking baby talk!

When he started this treatment with their first-born, Aissa, Pilar protested. She was sure he was spoiling her rotten.

"I can spoil the baby, but you can't," Duke retorted cheerfully. "Sorry, you'll have to be the villain." And he went right on cuddling and cooing and buying teddy bears.

Another Wayne practice that raised a lot of eyebrows was showing off his children from the time they were born. He took them to the set and put them in his pictures as soon as they could toddle.

Naming no names—but you probably know who they are—a lot of stars sounded off about "shielding children from the spotlight" and self-righteously refused to let them be photographed or visit the set or other places where they might be caught by the candid camera. In all fairness, some were genuinely afraid of kidnap threats of a child was recognized. But others didn't like it because the growing youngsters were an obvious commentary on their age.

"That's a lot of goddamn nonsense!" Duke snorted. Shrewdly, he felt that, given reasonable protection, a child who was easily recognized from photos had a better chance of being passed up by kidnappers, for just that reason. In any case, he'd never hide a child as if it had two heads. He was proud of his children and wanted them with him as much as possible.

He wanted them to become familiar with the business he loved, too. If they wanted to go into it, fine. If they didn't that was okay, too.

Duke always gives Josie lavish praise for the way his four older children have grown into fine, upstanding young people. "The burden was hers," he says (overlooking the fact that he worked at least twice as hard as other stars to provide all of them with the good things, including hefty trust funds). "She's a wonderful mother. And she's been very fair in allowing me to remain a part of their lives."

From the time they parted, Duke and Josie had a sensible, easygoing arrangement whereby the children stayed with her during the school year and spent summer vacations with him, wherever he might be. There were no hard and fast rules. Nor was there any of the bickering and bitterness that is so destructive to children of divorced parents.

Toni, then eight, was invited to a party where a

woman gushed, "What a lovely, good child you are! You must have a wonderful mother!"

Toni was bewildered. "My daddy's wonderful, too," she said.

Duke was delighted when he was able to take all four with him to Ireland in the summer of 1951 when he was making *The Quiet Man* there. And he was secretly tickled when fourteen-year-old Patrick buttonholed his godfather, who just happened to be the director, John Ford, and asked, "Uncle John, why don't you put us in the picture?" Naturally, they all wound up in front of the cameras and had a great time.

Visits with Dad weren't all fun. Working hard in his boyhood days had taught Duke some valuable lessons about the value of money, so sometimes he put the kids to work, doing such chores as opening mail in the offices of his Batjac company, and paid them according to what they produced.

He was secretly pleased when his eldest, Michael, got himself some summer jobs at the studios on his own, first as a messenger at M-G-M. He never told anyone who his father was, and he didn't tell his dad, either, that he was working at the studios because he didn't want him to know. He was determined to make good without the mixed blessing of being known as John Wayne's son.

Of course, this couldn't go on too long, and the truth came out when his dad asked him to go along on a wonderful location trip.

"I—I don't know if I can," Mike faltered.

"What d'you mean, you don't know?" Duke demanded. "What in the world's stopping you?"

Mike knew he had to face up to it. He gulped. "I—I'll have to ask my boss," he confessed.

Duke couldn't have been a happier man, ever, than he was at that moment—not merely because his son was showing such a genuine interest in movie-making, but because he had told him the truth, and he knew how hard it was.

"That was the one big thing that Dad was very strict about with us," Michael remembers. "He used to tell us, 'No matter what you do, no matter what kind of problems you may have or what kind of trouble you may get into, I want you to come and talk it over with me, and I will do my very best to help you, in any way that I can. But—never, *never* lie to me! If you do, I'll have to turn my back on you, for good!'"

"It wasn't just the serious way he said it that made a strong impression on us," Mike explains. "We knew he really meant it, because *he* never lied to *us*—or anybody, for that matter."

There was only one other rule that Duke laid down for his kids: No matter what they chose to do afterward, they had to finish school. He still remembered his own bitter disappointment when he was unable to finish college, and he was determined that his children, who certainly had the means to go, wouldn't foolishly throw away that opportunity and regret it later.

So the Wayne kids kept on cracking the books dutifully, even though their futures were already beckoning. Toni and Melinda, who'd grown into striking young beauties, were already being besieged by hopeful swains. And both boys, grinding away at Loyola University, knew where they were headed.

Unlike Mike, who was fascinated by the business

end of movie-making, Patrick felt more and more drawn to acting. Unlike both Mike and his dad, Patrick was sensitive and shy, dark and very handsome. If they didn't know it, no one would have guessed he was John Wayne's son.

That fact, plus Pat's good looks, made quite an impression on movie producers, naturally. While he was still in college, he was being offered parts and happily accepted them, with dad's blessing—as long as they didn't interfere with school.

One day, Duke got a call from his good friend, Gary Cooper. "I've seen Pat on the screen," he said, "and he's good, Duke—real good. I'd like to offer him a long-term contract, but I wanted to check it out with you, first."

For once, Duke was floored. It was the kind of chance young actors—including himself at that age—eat their hearts out for. But he knew what he had to say.

"You go ahead and put it up to him, Coop," he said. "He's the one who has to decide—not me."

Pat turned it down, without any hesitation. It would have meant that he would have had to quit school, and he wouldn't hurt his father by doing that for the world.

Pat has acted in many a film since—his dad's, and others. He's never been sorry he made that decision. "When I was in school," he says, "I really wasn't sure what I wanted to do. When I was in my teens, I went through a stage where I was sure I wanted to become a priest. When I got to be a little older, I realized it was just one of those teenage dreams you have, and I wasn't suited for it.

"I was in college when I decided that what I wanted, more than anything, was to become a good actor."

Pat laughs when he recalls telling his father about his intentions. Of course, he expected Dad to come up with all kinds of advice that would be helpful on his road to success.

"I'm really serious, Dad," Pat assured him. "I want to learn everything about acting."

It set Duke back on his heels—for a minute. Then he came up with what Pat still considers the perfect answer.

"Son," said his father, "I'm going to give you just four words of advice. They're all I'm ever going to give you, and they're all you'll ever need: *Listen to the director*!"

If he "spoiled" his children when they were little, when they were older Duke didn't leave all the discipline to Mama. Since he was away so much of the time, it wasn't easy, but he hit on a method that was very effective. "If any of us did something he didn't approve of," Melinda recalls, "he'd give us the Silent Treatment. He just avoided us and wouldn't talk to us. We couldn't stand it! Because all our lives he poured out love and attention to all of us, equally, we'd never deliberately do anything to risk losing it. In no time, we'd be terribly penitent—and all was forgiven. And you can believe we'd never do the same thing again!"

Melinda's sister Toni, four years older, was the first of Duke's daughters to marry. She'd met a bright young law student, Don LaCava, who was the nephew of the noted director, Gregory LaCava. After a hitch as a Navy aviator in Korea, Don was attending Loyola University with her brothers, Mike and Pat. The two of them fell madly in love.

Oddly enough, Don fulfilled two of Duke's lost

ambitions—to serve in the Navy and to become a lawyer. It could be that it had something to do with her dad's approval of Don, to the extent of relaxing his firm "finish college" stand to allow Toni to drop out of her last year at Immaculate Heart College to marry Don.

Naturally, once the date was set, the big guy who used to shower her with teddy bears went all out to make Toni's wedding the most perfect, beautiful, gorgeous, etc., etc., that any bride could possibly desire. And he succeeded admirably, though when the great day came he was far more nervous than the bride and groom. In fact, he was a total wreck!

More than 500 guests, including some of the movie colony's most distinguished names, came to the Blessed Sacrament Church, where the archbishop of Los Angeles, James Cardinal McIntyre, was to perform the ceremony, followed by a nuptial Mass.

Among them, none were more thrilled than two ladies—Toni's grandmother, Molly Morrison, and the good friend who had been bridesmaid at her parents' wedding—Loretta Young.

Toni and Don got through the ceremony happily and serenely, and somehow, her nervous father did, too. At last, he was able to relax at the lavish reception at the Beverly Hills Hotel and see the newlyweds off on a honeymoon in Acapulco.

The year was 1956. Aissa, the first child born to Duke and Pilar, was only a few months old. Two years later, Aissa became an aunt to Toni's first child, Maria Antonia.

That was only the beginning. Mike, Pat and Melinda also married, and now the total number of Wayne grandchildren has passed twenty, with no end in sight.

Nowadays, it's unusual to see John Wayne, on the set or off, without some little ones clambering around. If anyone calls him on the phone, the small voices in the background aren't telephone interference, they're just small children, making a sucker out of their grandfather, who loves every minute of it.

Just how important this part of his life is to him can be seen on the walls of his den. Just as prominent as the "Box Office Champion" plaques are the carefully framed mementos from his children, like little poems Toni and Melinda wrote when they were children.

One isn't on display, but it's deeply cherished by Pilar and Duke. It is a letter written to them by their daughter, Aissa, now seventeen, for no particular occasion—just a thank-you letter to them "for teaching me the values of truth and dignity."

As far as Duke is concerned, there isn't any "magic formula" that produced his untroubled teens. "Young people have respect for me as I have for them," he says simply, "so we get along fine. It's not an arm's length sort of thing. We can sit down and talk. All this permissiveness hasn't seemed to me to affect the younger generation as much as the blue-noses would expect."

In 1964, one of those young people, very dear to him, his daughter Melinda, was going to be married. At twenty-three, Melinda had also fallen in love with a lawyer—Gregory Robert Munoz, who, at twenty-six, was Los Angeles County deputy district attorney. Of course, a wedding as elaborate as Toni's was planned at the Blessed Sacrament Church with Cardinal McIntyre presiding at the ceremony and nuptial Mass.

Having been through it once, Duke wasn't quite so nervous when he gave his second daughter away, and the wedding went off without a hitch. When Melinda started to faint while kneeling through the nuptial Mass, Duke was quick to quietly rush up and steady her before she fell, and a priest brought a chair for her to sit on through the rest of the service.

On that happy day, no one knew that Duke was the one who was ill—seriously ill. Or that he had put off a date with the doctor because he didn't want to risk having anything spoil Melinda's wedding.

Chapter 12

ROUND ONE WITH THE BIG C

"I licked the Big C because they operated on me in time. They were able to remove it all. I was advised not to say anything, that it would destroy my image. Hell, there's a lot better image in a John Wayne who licked cancer! I'm going to tell my story, and go on telling it, so people will know how important it is to go for checkups, and get treatment in time!"

At fifty-seven, John Wayne had never been sick a day in his life. Oh, maybe a touch of grippe or virus now and then, but nothing bad enough to keep him

EXCLUSIVE PHOTO ALBUM

A tear for the tough guy—Duke is overcome as he accepts the Academy Award for "True Grit" in 1970, a crowning achievement of over 50 years in films. "It is my life and I love it," he says simply.

Marion Michael Morrison, age 5, with little brother Bobby near their Iowa home. Through the years since Marion became famous as John Wayne, the brothers remained close.

A cherished photo from Duke's memory book—"X" marks the helmet of the starring guard of the "Lightweight Champions of Central League." His prowess on this Glendale High team won him a scholarship at the University of Southern California.

In a rare, straight romantic role, in *Three Girls Lost,* (1931), the young John Wayne poses with long-time friend Loretta Young— Wayne's wedding to Josie Saenz took place in her home.

The early American west IS John Wayne. Here he poses in his role in *Alleghany Uprising* a 1939 RKO Radio film, directed by William Seiter.

Before the 1939 success of *The Stagecoach,* Wayne worked as journeyman actor for Monogram and other studios along "Poverty Row" in Hollywood. His star-quality showed even in these "B" pictures— and John Ford was just waiting to make his move.

In 1939 "Stagecoach" made him a star! A great, classic western, director John Ford insisted Duke play the leading role. "I owe everything to his belief in me," says Duke. "Our friendship has been the most profound relationship of my life."

Wayne with second wife, Esperanza "Chata" Baur, just after the private marriage ceremony on January 17, 1946. The marriage started out in church and ended up in court six years later.

"I'm not good enough," was Duke's reaction when Ford talked him into playing the Swedish sea captain in "The Long Voyage Home," (1940) based on plays by Eugene O'Neill. The film won critical acclaim, including rare praise from O'Neill himself!

As Thomas Dunson in *Red River* (1948), with Montgomery Clift, who was making his screen debut. This was the first time The Duke worked with director Howard Hawks.

John Wayne's stature as an actor has often been buried by routine scripts. One exception was his sensitive portrayal of an aging cavalry officer in "She Wore a Yellow Ribbon," 1950.

Duke put his heart and soul—and everything he owned—into his first venture as producer-director of "The Alamo," (1960) a personal statement of his belief in the values that made America great.

In triple role of producer-director-actor, Duke gets more than his feet wet as he lines up a shot for "The Green Berets" (1968). Pounded by the critics of the Vietnam war, the film was a huge financial success.

As whiskey-swilling Rooster Cogburn, who shows he has "True Grit" by taking the reins in his teeth and attacking the varmints with both guns blazing, Duke at last won Oscar recognition in 1970.

The Duke with his young cast in *The Cowboys* (1972), one of the rare movies in which his character dies on screen. But, as the boys in the film say, "It's how you're remembered" that counts.

With James Stewart in *The Shootist*, released in 1976. Some wonder if The Duke designed this to be his last movie, with its opening cuts from many of his finest westerns, and the plot concerning an aging gunslinger with cancer. It was a resounding critical success—but no one wants to hear the "last word" on the Duke.

John Wayne's youngest son, John Ethan, made his acting debut in THE MILLION DOLLAR KIDNAPPING. In this 1970 film, John Ethan plays the Duke's grandson.

The Duke has always enjoyed having his kids on the set—and letting them get into the act! Here's Pat Wayne with his famous Dad sharing a moment between scenes during the filming of RIO GRANDE (1950).

Wed since 1954, parents of three, Duke and his third wife, Peruvian beauty Pilar Palette, share his Oscar triumph.

His youngest, Marisa Carmela, makes her camera debut in 1966. Total Wayne children and grandchildren now number 20—and there is no end in sight.

Many faces, but always The Duke, in (clockwise from upper left): The Alamo (1960), The Conquerors (1956), True Grit (1969) and In Harm's Way (1965).

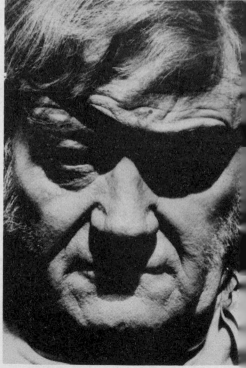

down. An ulcer—that ultimate credential of success in the movie industry—didn't keep him down, either. When it kicked up a little, he'd just switch from Scotch to soda for a while, and all would be well.

It was early in 1963 when the coughing spells started to get bad. By the time he finished *Donovan's Reef*, Pilar was really worried.

"Aw, it's nothing," he said. "Did I ever tell you about that bad cough my dad had before he came out here? The change of climate cleared it up right away!"

"But we *are* living in California!" Pilar pointed out. "I think you ought to see a doctor."

"Haven't got time," Duke said. "We start shooting *McLintock* in Nogales next week. Hey—why don't you come along? And bring Aissa—there's a great little part for her."

Pilar was relieved. Now, she wouldn't have to think of some lame excuse, or be a nagging wife, to go along and look after him.

They had a fine time in Nogales, and Pilar was pleased when Duke good-naturedly agreed to cut down on smoking, at her suggestion.

It didn't help.

Those who look at the exciting, glamorous finished products don't realize that movie-making is very tedious, painstaking work. Especially for the actors and actresses, who work themselves into a high emotional pitch for a scene, then have to come to a dead stop while somebody corrects the light, camera angles, or some other essential detail. These interruptions are bound to be nerve-wracking, and the stars usually hit on some "crutch" that will keep them from gnawing their nails until they get the signal to go back into action. (For years, Joan Crawford would walk off a set where Clark Gable or some equally romantic screen idol had been making mad love to her—and pick up her knitting.)

Duke, a high-strung, "let's get on with it" type to begin with, found his "crutch" in smoking. Whenever a break occurred, he'd light up a cigarette to relieve the tension.

As the pressures of his work increased, so did his smoking, especially since he was carrying the added burdens of producer as well as star. He was unable to relax at all during breaks, but had to check on what the trouble was instead of standing idly by waiting for the cameras to roll.

By the time he got to Nogales, he was smoking five packs of unfiltered cigarettes a day. He'd been smoking steadily for years, enjoyed it, and was sincere when he gave his endorsement for cigarette ads.

The dry, rasping cough persisted. "Maybe it's the dust in those riding scenes. Maybe I've been using my voice too hard," he'd say. Anything but smoking.

By the time he got back to Hollywood, he knew something was very wrong, and it had to be faced, sooner or later. Still, he kept stalling. "I just can't take care of it now," he'd tell Pilar. "I've got commitments. I have to do *The Greatest Story Ever Told* and, after that, I promised Otto Preminger I'd do *In Harm's Way*. And there's Melinda's wedding. I'm not going to take a chance of lousing that up!"

By the time he got through Melinda's wedding, everybody—including Duke—knew there couldn't be any more stalling. He checked into Scripp's Clinic in

La Jolla. Patiently—or as patiently as possible for him—he went through all the tests and X-rays. He was still positive that it was all a lot of fuss over something very minor. What could be wrong with a big, healthy guy like him?

In their usual casual manner, the doctors told him the truth without making it sound alarming. ''There's a suspicious spot on the X-rays, in your left lung. You'll have to go into Good Samaritan Hospital for further exploration and possible surgery.''

Before Duke could protest, he was whisked into the hospital.

His son, Michael, who by that time—September 1964—had taken over the production reins at his dad's company, Batjac, knew even less than Duke. When word got around that John Wayne was in the hospital, reporters put poor Mike on the spot.

Gamely, Mike came up with a story. His dad had pulled a tendon in his ankle when he was making *Legend of the Lost* and had to have it corrected before he went into their next picture, *The Sons of Katie Elder*, which was a very strenuous Western.

When he learned more of the details, Mike—the boy his father had taught never to lie—lamely admitted that there was ''a respiratory complication.'' Asked for particulars, he explained that it was ''an infection, an abcess of some kind.'' Things like this happened in hospitals, Mike went on and, to back it up, gave them the story of his own experience, when he and brother Pat had been in an auto accident and he got a broken leg. ''I wound up with gout and what they called a pulmonary embolism,'' Mike said. ''You never know . . .''

123

Mike had predicted the length of his dad's hospital stay would be a week. When that stretched into two, the reporters decided that somebody wasn't telling them everything. The family was either covering up—or awfully ignorant.

The truth was that although Mike, along with everyone else, had strong suspicions that the "abcess" was cancer, it wasn't confirmed by the doctors. So Mike stuck to his story, determined to protect his father at all costs until the doctors saw fit to tell *him* exactly what it was.

It wasn't easy. The delay that aroused the reporters' doubts had been caused by an unexpected complication. After the first operation, Duke had a coughing spell that broke the newly repaired tissues, causing the lung—and the rest of him—to blow up like a balloon filled with fluid. He had to be rushed back for a second operation within five days.

After that, they put him in Intensive Care. There, Duke's former strength and spirit made a big comeback in a few days—goaded by the sight of severely ill cardiac patients around him. Not that he wasn't sympathetic; he just couldn't stand the idea of being so helpless himself. After ten days, he was ready to crawl up the walls.

"If you don't get me out of here," he told the doctors and nurses, "I'm going to get a gun and shoot my way out!"

For fear he might get carried away and break some more tissue, they quickly transferred him to a private room on another floor.

Once established there, his improvement was rapid. In a short time he was able to sit up and receive visitors—and speak for himself. From the time he'd entered the hospital, he'd been under heavy sedation. Once he was out of it, he was ready to talk and take on all comers.

To everybody, including members of the press, he gave all the details he knew of the two operations—except whether the "thing" they had removed was cancer.

He certainly didn't look, or act, as if he'd been through any such great crisis. A newspaperman who visited him reported that he watched in amazement while Big John consumed a large bowl of soup, several pork chops with vegetables and salad, a huge piece of pie and coffee.

"You can see we have one big problem with this patient," the nurse quipped. "He has such a poor appetite!"

By that time, Duke was as suspicious as everybody else about the real nature of his illness. In typical Wayne style, he called in his doctors.

"Now, I want you to tell me the whole truth," he demanded. "Don't lie to me."

"They knew me damn well enough to know they hadn't better," he chuckled later. "They told me that it was the Big C, but that I'd licked it. Because I'd come to them in time, they were able to remove it completely."

It was a great relief, to him and to his family and friends, to have all the doubts removed, too. Only those close to him knew the private agony he was going through in spite of his brave, cheerful front.

"Anybody's bound to be affected by a threat of cancer," a close friend says, "but that wasn't the thing that got Duke the most. What hurt him was that he'd never been hospitalized, or even really sickly in his life, and he thought nothing like that would ever happen to him. When it did, it was a hard blow. For the first time, he had to admit to himself that he wasn't invulnerable.''

In the weeks ahead, he had to decide whether he should make a much bigger admission. He'd finally come to terms, and overcome, the dangers to his physical well-being. What he had to face now was a crisis of conscience: Should he tell the public that he, John Wayne, always the strong, fearless and conquering hero, had been operated on for cancer?

His business associates, who had a lot of money riding on the box-office appeal of John Wayne, strongly advised against it. "It's suicide, Duke," they told him. "It's going to destroy your public image. Anyway, why bother? The doctors told you they got it all, and you'll be okay. Why not just let the whole thing blow over?"

It wasn't just the money he was thinking about. He'd been broke plenty of times and got back on his feet again. But he knew that this was different. A whole lot of people depended on him, in a lot of ways—not just his family, but people in the business, right down to some little guy who made a buck running John Wayne films in a small-town movie house.

When he was released from the hospital on October 8, he was still wrestling with the problem. He'd lost weight, but looked fit and faced the reporters, smiling.

Patiently, he answered questions about the operation.

Finally, one newsman blurted out the big question in all their minds: "Do you have cancer?"

Duke kept right on smiling. "I guess not," he said, quite honestly.

Later, Pilar explained what happened during that difficult time. "We never lie," she said. "Up to a point, of course, we really didn't know. When we did, after it was all over, the question still was, 'Does he have cancer?' We could honestly say no, because the doctors had assured us that they got it all out. If they had asked if he had *had* cancer, I don't know what we would have done."

Convalescing in his Encino home, Pilar could hear him pacing back and forth in his den. "He always does that when there's something he's trying to work out in his mind," she says.

It didn't take him very long to work it out. After a few weeks' rest he was back in his old fighting form and ready to do what he knew he had to do—regardless of the consequences. Defying his advisers, he called the press. Columnist Earl Wilson in New York got the scoop on the story, which was spread throughout the world in headlines.

"They told me it was going to hurt my image if I told people I had cancer," Duke said. "I decided there's a hell of a lot better image in a John Wayne who licked the Big C.

"Film image or not, I think I ought to tell my story so other people can be saved by getting annual checkups. I was very fortunate because it was detected early enough. I finally decided that if I, John Wayne, came out and said something about cancer, it might stop some poor slob from putting a gun in his mouth and blowing his brains out.''

Contrary to all the dire predictions, the story didn't hurt his career one bit. Since that day in 1964, nothing has given him greater satisfaction that being a living example to those who have to face their own fights with cancer.

Two months after he got out of the hospital, he was back at work in Durango, Mexico, on *The Sons of Katie Elder*, as strenuous a Western as any he had ever made.

"The docs okayed me for this picture, and my insurance rates haven't gone up," he'd point out, proudly. To anybody interested, he'd show his "scar"—a thin, 18-inch long line running from his left breast, swinging under his armpit and back to his left shoulder blade.

The toughest part of the whole ordeal had to be faced next. He couldn't use smoking as a "crutch" on the set anymore.

He tried candy, munching his way steadily through quantities of Vicks cough drops, Allenberg's Pastilles, chocolate-covered almonds, Wrigley's spearmint gum, and the entire stock of peppermint wafers in the local *dulceria*.

It was enough to make more sensitive stomachs rebel (including those of his co-workers) but somehow he got through it. Like many former smokers, he has continued to succumb to an occasional cigarette—and has even been known to "chaw" during hectic location work. But the five packs a day habit was a thing of the past.

After any cancer operation, the first five years are considered the danger period. Duke went through those five years, continuing to work regularly and strenuously, though he did ease his commitments. He tried to keep his actual working time down to five months a year. Even Duke Wayne had to make some concessions to the Big C. Shortly after leaving the hospital, he admitted with his usual honesty, "My interests are as varied and wide but my energy is down. I have to use will power now—before I couldn't find enough to do to get tired." That will power, combined with his naturally hardy constitution and the help of The Man Upstairs, helped him pass the critical first five years with flying colors. Duke had his moments of doubt. In 1974 he told an interviewer, "I haven't quite gotten over the feeling that I'm pretty much living on borrowed time." But the doubt was lightened by more positive feelings: gratitude and hope.

Chapter 13

THE ROUGH ROAD TO RECOVERY

"I know I went back to work too soon. But hell, I can't stand sitting around. I've got to get back to work. And now, I realize how precious life is. There are a lot of things I want to do, and I don't want to waste a minute of it."

<hr/>

When Duke went back to work in *The Sons of Katie Elder* two months after his cancer operation, his doctors were horrified. They told him that he would have to have a long rest, at least six months, before he made another movie.

"I know I came back too soon," he admitted, "but I had to. Hell, I can't stand being idle. I've got to get back to work."

The filming was done in Durango, Mexico, in an isolated spot across the border from Texas that his company had already acquired because it had the untouched atmosphere of the old West. There, he reconstructed an entire town as it would have appeared in those days, authentic down to the last detail.

The Mexicans, in Durango and in Mexico City, where he filmed interior shots at Churubusco Studios, had come to regard him as a benevolent saint on horseback who showered them with the blessings of prosperity. *"El Macho"* they called him—'The Manly One."

For him the blessings of cheap Mexican labor weren't the big attraction. All expenses considered, he could make the same pictures at a much lower cost near Hollywood. Besides, Durango, without question, is one of the most uncomfortable places in the world. At an altitude of 8,000 feet, the air is thin and the temperature seesaws from freezing cold by night to broiling sun by day.

So why Durango? And why should he rush back to that godforsaken country against doctors' orders?

The answers to those questions explain a lot that isn't understood about John Wayne, the man and the actor.

"Durango isn't phony," he'll tell you, simply. "It's one place that's still pretty much untouched. The country there gives you the feeling that it must have been the same many years ago, when the kind of action you see in Westerns today was a reality."

Reality is what he's after—in the rugged terrain,

131

uncluttered by telephone poles and motel signs, in the Mexican extras who can still roll their own and shoot from the hip—and in himself.

When he went back there to make *The Sons of Katie Elder*, he was testing himself. He *had* to find out whether he could make it, for his own satisfaction.

Pilar came to be near him and keep a watchful eye on him. She brought little John Ethan, whose antics tickled the whole cast as well as his doting dad.

One morning, Dean Martin, co-starring with Duke in the film, came on the set without his spurs. "Mr. Martin," John Ethan announced seriously, "you forgot your propellers!"

Duke got through the film with nothing more than a few extra whiffs from the handy oxygen tank, always ready to counteract the effects of the too-thin air. Mounting a horse caused excruciating pain on his left side, betrayed by only a slight wince. Nobody dared suggest that he use a stand-in.

Ironically, in his next film, *Cast a Giant Shadow*, filmed in Italy, he was really badly hurt in a way that had nothing whatever to do with his operation. There was a scene in which Duke and Kirk Douglas were in a jeep, fighting over Angie Dickinson. Duke suddenly crumpled in pain and was rushed to the hospital. The X-rays showed he'd suffered a slipped disc. He was forced to stay in the hospital and rest for three days, then he was released with the order that he rest in bed a few more days.

"Hell, let's get this picture finished," he told the director, as soon as he was outside the hospital door. "I want to get home!"

He had a good reason. Pilar was expecting their third

child any day. He got back in time to make his third trip to St. Joseph's and welcome another child, little Marisa Carmela on February 22, 1966—John Ethan's fourth birthday.

In his next picture he was teamed with Robert Mitchem in *El Dorado*, a Howard Hawks production. Then he went back to Durango for *War Wagon*, with Kirk Douglas.

Duke still regards that picture as one of his better efforts, and laments the fact that "the Cannes festival wanted to show it, but the studio chickened out." Despite its considerable merits, *War Wagon* was notable chiefly for a private war waged between Duke and Kirk Douglas.

Ronald Reagon was running for Governor of California and, throughout the movie industry, feelings pro and con ran high.

When Kirk walked out of *War Wagon* in the middle of production to make a TV trailer against Reagan, Duke was livid.

"Goddamn it, Old Dimple-chin isn't going to get away with this," Duke declared. When Kirk got back, he had to sit and cool his heels on the set—because Duke had gone off to make a TV trailer *for* Reagan!

Both of them were too professional to let the run-in interfere with their work, so when Duke came back the "war" simmered down to good-natured banter. At one point, the two were supposed to kill a pair of gunmen coming at them.

"Mine hit the ground first," Kirk crowed.

"Mine was taller," Duke retorted.

No matter how far he may roam to make movies,

Durango is home base to Duke. It's more than an ideal place to make Westerns. It's the place where he can "get away from it all" and get back to simple, uncomplicated values in a world that, for him, is becoming more and more complex, with a million and one demands on his time and energy. It's a retreat where he can relax and get back his perspective.

Undoubtedly, during that recovery period from his cancer operation, it helped him through a rough time.

Strenuous as it was, the work he had to do was the best therapy. It took his mind off the inner doubts and fears that must beset every cancer patient. The five-year "wait and see" period was particularly hard for him. For the first time, he was up against something he couldn't tackle head-on. It was like the threat of an elusive gunman, always hiding just out of reach, always menacing.

He was pushing sixty, and some of his best friends were already gone. Victor McLaglen, who'd played with him in many a scene, including one of the best knockdown, drag-out fights of all time in *The Quiet Man*. Ward Bond, who died of a heart attack in 1960, just when he was coming back strong on TV in *Wagon Train* after a long period of being ostracized by Hollywood studios because of his membership in the Motion Picture Alliance for the Preservation of American Ideals, in which Duke was also very active. Clark Gable—how well Duke understood his genuine love of movie-making! "As long as they let me creep onto a set," he used to say, "I'll go on creeping!" At least, he'd had the satisfaction of being in there, a top star, right to the day the fatal heart attack cut him down. Gary Cooper. Coop was a big star when Duke was still falling off horses in third-rate Westerns. The Big C got him. Why? *Why*? Why should *he* be any different from these men, his friends, who certainly deserved to live as much as he did. Why should *he* be the lucky one?

Then again, maybe he wasn't so lucky. They had told him he'd licked the Big C, but could you really know?

Reassurance came unexpectedly when famed Dr. Charles W. Mayo of the Mayo Clinic traveled all the way to Mexico City to bestow a special citation for "doing a wonderful job in combatting the cancer phobia."

Dr. Mayo, a leading cancer specialist, said that Duke's efforts in warning people about cancer and urging them to have checkups, because such a checkup saved his life, had a far better effect on people than any doctor's advice. "When we tell them, they think we're just looking for business," Dr. Mayo said. "When John Wayne tells them, they listen!"

From then on, Duke was able to forget his own doubts. If Dr. Mayo had such confidence in his recovery and the job he was trying to do to fight cancer, then he wasn't going to let him down. He redoubled his work on behalf of the cause, and the Mayo citation was the first of many he received.

The time he spent in Durango had helped him to kick the smoking habit, too. There, he was able to wrestle it out alone, free from constant temptation. There, with only his cast and crew and family—all of them knowing what he was going through and respecting it—he was able to reach the point where he would never touch a cigarette again.

Through it all, he had one big motivation.

"Life is very precious to me now," he said. "I want to spend more time with my family and doing the things that are really important to me. I don't want to waste a minute."

As his pace increased, everyone marveled that a man who'd had a rib and most of one lung cut out could possibly go on like that without collapsing.

To anybody who asked him about it, Duke had a standard reply.

"Well, you see, it's this way," he'd say, his face breaking into the familiar, crooked grin. "I've got big lungs!"

Chapter 14

"HELL, I'M NO ACTOR!"

"I don't act—I react. Whatever part I'm playing, whether it be a cowboy, pilot or sea captain, I always have to be John Wayne, just living through the experience. And the people who see me on the screen live it along with me."

Over the years, Durango hasn't changed, and John Wayne hasn't either.

He's up at five in the morning, conditioned by years of the movie-making routine that decrees actors and actresses must report for makeup at the crack of dawn to save time and money when the rest of the crew is ready to go, later.

His breakfast is huge and, like most of his meals, features a fine cut of New York steak, rare. Also eggs, toast, fruit and coffee, all in considerable quantities.

He's usually the first one on the set, ready to submit to the makeup man's ministrations. In spite of having gone through this thousands of times, he still approaches it with the pained distaste of a little boy confronted by a large dose of castor oil.

He slumps into a chair, surrendering himself to Web Overlander, the makeup expert who's been with him for many years and is a close friend as well as co-worker.

"Good news today, Duke" Web tells him. "All the scenes are outside, so you don't have to wear the hairpiece."

"Thank God," Duke mutters.

Ever since his hair started thinning on top, he's had to put up with the hated hairpiece for indoor shots. Outdoor shots mean he can just cram on his old sweat-stained Stetson and feel perfectly comfortable.

In Durango, especially, but also in other places with strange climates, Web's job is protective rather than prettifying. To keep the fierce Mexican sun from broiling Duke to a point where he looks like one of his favorite rare steaks before the week is out, Web has to take all precautions.

First, he works Nivea cream generously into his face and jowls and neck. Then he gets to work on his chest and back, smearing on an evil-smelling concoction. Last, he gives the muscles in Duke's legs a good rubdown with Absorbine Jr., to alleviate the pain of past injuries and reduce the chance of cramps during rugged riding.

So much for the makeup. Duke is ready to go into action.

"Actors aren't really dead," Web tells him brightly. "They just smell that way."

"I'll get you tonight at poker!" Duke threatens, and lopes off to the set in that peculiar, long, slightly pigeon-toed stride that has become as much a John Wayne trademark as the Stetson.

He's usually the first one there, but it's a matter of habit rather than being "the boss" checking up on everything, although, as head of the company, that's what he is. Long years before the cameras had taught him that, in making a movie, the only boss must be the director.

Often, his directors are old pros like Henry Hathaway. Duke feels a real kinship to Henry, not only because he admires his ability, but because he helped him through his cancer crisis by telling him that he'd been operated on for cancer of the stomach at the Mayo Clinic and hadn't had a recurrence in twelve years!

Another of his favorite directors is Andy McLaglen, Victor's son. The fact that he's known Andy since he was a little tyke doesn't diminish Duke's respect for his talent. He gladly takes Andy's direction any time, and only wishes his old man had lived to see his son's success.

Wayne films are always a "family affair" because Duke likes to have his family and friends around him at work. Son Mike, of course, is usually there, having taken over more and more of the production responsibilities. If Pat happens to have a part in the picture, he's on hand, too.

Duke's favorite pastime while waiting to go before the cameras is playing chess with one of his sons. Sometimes he becomes so engrossed in these games that he has to be called several times before the message sinks through that he's wanted.

His brother, Bob Morrison, was a frequent member of the group until his death at age 58 of cancer. Bob was a big, good-looking guy who strongly resembled Duke, though he was more quiet and reserved in temperament. Acting had never had any appeal for him at all, but he did well on the technical side of moviemaking, and he worked often on the production or directing end of the Duke's movies. Bob fought the same battle his older brother had fought several years before him; the two brothers had both faced the Big C at a comparatively early age. But on July 25, 1968, Bob Morrison had succumbed.

The Wayne entourage includes a lot of people the public never heard of, like makeup artist Web Overlander. They are there because Duke regards them as close, trusted friends as well as seasoned co-workers, and there's a strong bond of loyalty between them.

Some of his friends feel that Duke's loyalty goes too far. He's a sucker for a hard-luck story, and his pictures usually manage to include a few needy actors who have turned up because one of his friends sent them.

Once, one of these poor souls was featured in a scene where he was supposed to shoot Duke in the stomach. The fellow, as usual, had no acting recommendation except that he was a friend of a friend.

Patiently, Duke went through the scene with him

again and again. Each time Duke had to take a bad tumble in the dirt, and his crew was perturbed about the mounting cost. The scene, which should have been done in a couple of takes, was costing thousands of dollars.

When it was finally finished, the director called Duke aside. "For God's sake," he demanded, "why'd you do a fool thing like that?"

Duke grinned sheepishly. "The guy just doesn't know how to shoot somebody in the stomach," he explained, as if that settled everything.

Shooting somebody in the stomach, or any other way, and making it look convincing is just one of the items in Duke's bag of acting tricks. Those years of toiling in bargain basement horse operas gave him a savvy in outdoor action scenes and indoor brawls that very few actors have today. He's quick to give the credit for his knowledge to the stuntmen he worked with in those days, particularly his close friend, Yakima Canutt—"the greatest stuntman who ever lived."

Be that as it may, few critics would fail to give him his due as a master of action scenes, whether he's in them or directing them. Unfortunately, when it comes to his acting in other areas, it's a different story. For years, it's seemed that a favorite sport among film critics is seeing who can come up with the most devastating description of John Wayne's acting.

Duke has always shrugged it off. "I know my political philosophy isn't popular with a lot of those pinkos," he says, "but it's never stopped people from coming to see my pictures. It's never hurt me at the box office, so who cares?"

Actually, his political philosophy isn't entirely responsible for this "John Wayne is a lousy actor" attitude. To a great extent, Duke has brought it on himself because he is his own worst detractor.

For years, he's been proclaiming, "I'm not an actor. I don't act—I react."

When young hopefuls ask him for advice, he'll tell them, "All I can say is don't start the way I did. I knocked around for a long time and learned from experience, but I'm sure that leaves a lot to be desired, and it's not the best way. Get a good education, then go to a good dramatic school if you're serious about it. You'll be better prepared than I was."

There *are* a few people around who have a high regard for John Wayne's acting talents—the directors who've worked with him.

"I wish that big idiot would stop going around telling everybody he can't act," growled John Ford. "He's one hell of a fine actor!"

Only once did one of the blistering reviews get him hot under the collar, and that was because he thought it made him look like an ignoramus, not just a bad actor.

The review, in *Time* magazine, covered *The Conqueror*, a huge RKO extravaganza in which Duke, as Genghis Khan, was totally miscast.

"He portrays the great conqueror as a sort of cross between a square-shootin' sheriff and a Mongolian idiot," the *Time* reviewer wrote. That wasn't all.

"Yer beeooduful in yer wrath," was the way Duke's dialogue sounded when he wooed Susan Hayward. "Know this, woman, I want you fer wife. All other wimmin are like the pressin- uh the grape."

It wasn't very consoling that the beautiful thoroughbred horses used in the picture came in for their share of blasting along with his performance, because only tough little Mongol ponies could survive in the freezing steppes.

"What gets me," Duke said, pacing back and forth as he always does when he's bothered, "is that the guy made me sound like an ignorant boob. Hell, I'm not that dumb! I had a high honor average in high school and in college. Why, when I started to make Westerns, they had to teach me to say ain't!"

True. Granted also, *The Conqueror* was certainly one of his lesser efforts. The unfortunate aspect of Duke's whole acting career is that, like his school record, his very impressive achievements tend to be overlooked or forgotten.

This is due mainly to the fact that no other actor can match his record in sheer quantity. There is no accurate record of the number of films John Wayne has starred in because even he can't remember! What is a known fact is that the total is now well past the 200 mark.

Of this staggering total, a great number can be considered really good and, as Duke would be the first to state, a lot were awful. But the fact usually overlooked is that John Wayne has starred in more films judged truly *great* by time and the critics than any other motion picture actor.

Obviously, since he carried the starring role, a large share of their greatness is due to his performance. More surprising, these roles are very varied, not merely a succession of gun-totin' cowboys.

Here is the list, an "Absolutely Don't Miss" guide

for not only Wayne fans, but anyone who appreciates the best in movies:

Stagecoach—Released by United Artists in March 1939, directed by John Ford. First of the great classic Westerns, and the picture that made John Wayne a first-rank star. His role as the Ringo Kid, unjustly accused of his father's murder, who has broken out of jail in pursuit of the real killers, strongly influenced his future screen image.

The Long Voyage Home—Released by United Artists in November 1940, directed by John Ford. Based on four one-act plays by Eugene O'Neill about the crew of a cargo boat awaiting the end of a voyage eagerly, only to be disillusioned when it comes. In a complete departure for him, Wayne played the part of Ole Olsen, a rough Swedish seaman. This widely acclaimed film was O'Neill's favorite among his works brought to the screen.

Fort Apache—Released by RKO in March 1948, directed by John Ford. Another great classic Western from John Ford, in which John Wayne gives one of his finest performances as an aide, frustrated by martinet colonel Henry Fonda's stupidity. Both are brilliant in this exciting, suspenseful film.

Red River—Released by United Artists in September 1948, directed by Howard Hawks. In this epic Western, all doubt is removed about John Wayne's stature as an actor. "He embues the aging cattleman, Tom Dunson, with his characteristic authority and, in addition, brings a kind of epic dignity to the role," wrote one reviewer. In his fiery exchanges with talented Montgomery Clift, who plays his son, he is unforgettable.

She Wore a Yellow Ribbon—Released by RKO in October 1949, directed by John Ford. Still another of the classic Ford Westerns. Again, Wayne turns in a very sensitive portrayal of an aging man, Captain Nathan Brittles, a U.S. Cavalry officer on his last mission before retirement—to defeat the Indians massed for Custer's Last Stand and avert a full-scale Indian war.

Sands of Iwo Jima—Released by Republic in March 1950, directed by Allan Dwan. Best of a number of films about World War II starring John Wayne, this one won him an Academy Award nomination for his role as a tough Marine sergeant leading untried men into battle. Authentic photography from the Marines and Navy is used with striking effect.

Rio Grande—Released by Republic in 1950, directed by John Ford. An unusual film because it is a sequel to *Fort Apache*, with Wayne playing Kirby York as a middle-aged man. It lives up to the high artistic values of the first film, and is outstanding for the depth and maturity of the relationship between Wayne and his screen wife, Maureen O'Hara.

True Grit—Released by Paramount in July 1969, directed by Henry Hathaway. At last, John Wayne won an Oscar for his most unflattering role—the rascally, mean, drunken, fat, one-eyed U.S. Marshal, Rooster Cogburn. Credit also goes to Henry Hathaway's fine direction of the whole production.

No one who sees all the films on the list above can fail to realize that John Wayne *is* a very fine actor, no matter what he says.

Though he certainly isn't given to making any

lengthy statements about his theories on acting, what little he has said makes a lot of sense and goes a long way to explain his success.

What does he mean by "I don't act, I react"?

"Screen acting is very different from stage acting," he says. "On the stage, the actors are completely apart from the audience. That situation calls for acting, in the accepted sense of the word, to put the play across. When the people watch a movie, the situation isn't the same. They feel that they are actually a *part* of what's going on onscreen, not watching from a distance. So the screen actor must project a genuine *reaction* to whatever confronts him in the scene. If he doesn't, if he tried to *act*, it's going to look phony."

The way he sees it, "I deal with basic emotions. I hate, I love, I get angry, I feel kind. This is what people want to do. They come and do it right along with me, or through watching me on the screen."

It's often been said that he plays himself, and he won't argue with that. "Whether I'm playing a cowboy, pilot, sea captain or Texas Ranger, I always have to be John Wayne, just living through the experience."

What movie audiences have experienced is an All-American hero exaggeration, whose superhuman courage and ideals are tempered with a rough good humor. It works because it *is* an exaggerated image of Duke himself.

"I'm just Old Honest Blue-Eyes, I guess," he says. "All I've got to sell is sincerity."

That sincerity, in action, means that he simply will not do anything on the screen that he feels is out of character, to the extent that he couldn't "react" sincerely to it. This does not mean that he always has to be heroic and idealistic. Far from it.

"I think I've always been popular in Westerns because I've played the kind of fellow who had a little bit of bad in him as well as a little bit of good, who had weaknesses," he says. "The only thing I've tried to stay away from is anything petty, or small, or mean."

He doesn't think that any actor worth his salt should stick to a script literally, but he should create his own interpretation of the character as he sees it. Only in this way can he give the role believability—or, to use his favorite word, sincerity.

Once a script put him in a situation where he was to act thoroughly frightened. He refused to play it the way it was written.

"Fear is a natural emotion," he explained, "but to have the character I was playing suddenly scared to death struck a false note. I could act scared, all right, but not lily-livered. There had to be a hint of courage in it. Otherwise, it wouldn't be right for me."

This strong instinct for what is right for him has stood him in good stead over the years. And as the years piled up, he never had any illusions about himself.

"My problem is that I'm not a handsome man like Cary Grant, who will still be handsome at sixty-five," he said. "I never want to play silly old men chasing young girls, as some of the stars are doing."

Cary Grant, incidentally, is John Wayne's favorite actor. He admires his superb acting technique, and possibly envies Grant's smooth sophistication, good looks and charm, although to those who know them, the two stars have the same strong personal magnetism that completely dominates any crowd they happen to be in.

Duke regrets about delegating himself to non-romantic roles. He never did relish screen lovemaking. "I kept thinking of all those people on the set watching," he says. "Then, I was always worried about squashing the girl's nose, and the mike overhead picking up the kiss so it sounds like a cow pulling her foot out of the mud. And the way they flavor that lipstick! It tastes like hot, stale raspberries! If those cosmetic guys would invent one that tastes like rare steak, they'd have something. God, I never enjoyed those love scenes one bit!"

His leading ladies have recorded a variety of reactions to the Duke. Patricia Neal and Natalie Wood remember him fondly. Lauren Bacall, his co-star in *Blood Alley* and also in the recent film *The Shootist*, has praised his easy-going courtesy and professionalism: "We had a marvelous working relationship." On the other hand, Lana Turner, asked for her opinion of John Wayne by a London newspaper in 1974, had "no comment."

In answer to the same newspaper's request that he describe La Turner, the Duke was characteristically generous—but honest: "Lana was the kind of girl who showed up at the Academy Awards and everyone knew they were seeing a real star. Whew! You don't know how difficult it was for me to say that!"

Janet Leigh was considerably younger than Wayne when they co-starred in the ill-fated *Jet Pilot*, and both of them looked considerably younger (as well as quite foolish) when the picture was released by its eccentric producer, Howard Hughes, eight years after it was made. (It seemed that Howard, the aviation expert, wanted to update the jet planes used, but finally just couldn't keep up with the rapid progress being made and had to release the picture as it was—with woefully dated planes.) The result, as one reviewer pointed out, "wasn't supposed to be a comedy, but Wayne and Leigh have never been funnier!"

One interviewer asked Janet if she had found her love scenes with John Wayne exciting.

"Well, no," she admitted, then added thoughtfully, "but he's very thorough!"

Chapter 15

LORD, HOW THE MONEY ROLLS IN! (AND OUT)

"I am not popular because I'm cheap–I get a pot of dough every time I make a picture. I suppose my best attribute, if you want to call it that, is sincerity. I can sell sincerity because that's the way I am. I can't be insincere or phony. I can't say a petty thing and make it sound right."

During one of those periodic slumps that send the whole motion picture industry into a state of panic, one top executive got tired of the general moaning and groaning and the feeble suggestions for curing the sick giant.

"There's nothing wrong with this business," he snorted, "that a dozen John Waynes couldn't cure!"

Nobody could argue with that. The facts backed him up, and sensational facts they are.

During the past forty years, John Wayne films have grossed well over 700 million dollars.

In 1949 he rose to the exalted status of the Top Ten on the list most revered by movie-makers—the *Motion Picture Herald* box-office poll. In 1950 and 1951 he was first on the list and has remained in the Top Ten ever since—a record unmatched by any other actor.

He is one of only three actors whose name on a contract will guarantee a million dollar loan from a bank to the producers (the other two are Paul Newman and Steve McQueen, who haven't enjoyed that rank nearly so long).

John Wayne has starred in 17 of the 100 highest grossing movies of all time. He has made more money for his studios than any other star. And a recent poll showed that more people recognize John Wayne's face than any other man in history except Abraham Lincoln.

Ever since John Wayne hit the top in 1950—and stayed there—people have been analyzing the reasons for his overwhelming popularity.

"He is shy with women, tough with men, violent and romantic by turns but, above all, has authority," one writer concluded.

Time magazine, in its first cover story on him, labeled him as a "trademark of incorruptibility."

The two directors who know him best, Raoul Walsh and John Ford, voiced similar opinions.

"From the first time I tested him," Walsh said, "I knew all he had to do was be himself. His looks, his manner, his personality made him a natural for motion pictures."

Said John Ford, "Boys and men admire him, and women love him, because he's a clean-cut, good-looking, virile, typically American type. They'd like to have him for a pal, a brother or a husband. When you watch him on the screen, he's not something out of a book, acting according to the rules. He's John Wayne, a rugged American guy. He's real."

According to Ford, this didn't mean that he isn't a good actor. "He's a great actor! So are Gary Cooper and Clark Gable, but all three are what I call natural actors, because they've played parts similar to their own characters. This isn't true of James Stewart, for instance, who is quite different from the familiar character he's created on the screen."

When anybody asks Duke himself for an explanation of his popularity, he'll just laugh and say, "Well, I figure I've been around so long that people think of me as one of the family."

He does have one theory, though. "I think it's the men who are responsible for my showing at the box office to a great extent. Say, a man comes home from work, dog-tired. His wife's tired, too, after a day of cooking and cleaning, and she'd like to get out of the house. 'Let's go to a movie,' she says. So the man looks in the paper, and the John Wayne movie is the only one he can stand because it has the kind of action men like. So that's what they go to see!"

He overlooks one factor. By 1950, when the big upsurge in his rank took place, he was appearing in pictures with more emphasis on the love interest, which certainly boosted his rating with women. He was also playing those scenes opposite some of the most glamorous names in the business—Lana Turner (*The Sea Chase*), Lauren Becall (*Blood Alley*), Susan Hayward (*The Conqueror*), Claudette Colbert (*Without Reservations*), Sophia Loren, (*Legend of the Lost*). And of course, the beautiful, redhead, Irish spitfire who was his "perfect screen wife"—Maureen O'Hara. Another John Ford find, Maureen was the ideal foil for a John Wayne, her fire and spirit pitted against his stoic strength. Teamed first in *Rio Grande*, they went into a hilarious, rough-and-tumble romance in *The Quiet Man*, then *Wings of the Eagles*, then *McLintock*, in which poor Maureen got thrown into a mudhole and had to flee from Big John by running down the main street in her underwear.

With all that money rolling into the box office, John Wayne must be fabulously wealthy—right? Wrong. The truth is that it wasn't until very recent years that he has been able to get on his feet financially, even though he's been in the high bracket class for a long time.

His business manager, Bo Roos, wasn't kidding when he testified at Duke's divorce trial that he wasn't nearly so rich as Chata believed (or, anyway, hoped). Before Roos came into the picture and put the lid on, Duke had been prone to taking flyers on business ventures that sounded great when their promoters told him about them over a few drinks. Some of these worked out but a lot of them didn't. "Duke must be the largest owner of defunct shrimp boat fleets in the world," a friend sighed.

In 1952, he had made a move to better his financial

position by forming his own production company in cooperation with Robert Fellows, who resigned his position as an RKO executive to set up Wayne-Fellows Productions.

Wayne was one of the first to grasp the advantages of a star becoming his own producer, an example many followed in later years to escape the "star system" for greater financial gains.

His lack of false ego had made him conclude, years before the first furrows appeared on his brow, that there would come a day when the public would no longer flock to see John Wayne.

On the sets, he would watch and learn from everybody. He learned why things were done a certain way, how to save money. People he really respected, like John Ford, he followed around like a big faithful hound dog, eyeing its master.

"Listen, you bum," Ford would bellow. "Why are you always hanging around, staring at me like that?"

"Just want to make sure you're not slipping a marked deck up your sleeve," Duke would snap back, grinning.

He began taking a hand in production in the forties, and got his first credit as co-producer of *Angel and the Badman* in 1947. More co-producing credits followed, until in 1952 he felt ready to take the plunge, with Fellows contributing his know-how from the business end.

His close watch on Ford had taught Duke one valuable lesson—that the best movie-making comes from close loyalty and teamwork. Gradually, he gathered around him artists and technicians whose talents were second to none.

One was writer-director James Edward Grant, who had worked with him on *Angel and the Badman* and *Flying Leathernecks* and wrote the script for *Bullfighter and the Lady*. The latter film was the first Wayne had done as full producer, and without himself in the starring role. That went to Robert Stack. It was so successful that Wayne was finally convinced that he was ready to "go into business on his own." Grant continued to do the writing on some of the most successful Wayne films, including *Hondo*, *The Alamo*, *The Comancheros* and *McLintock*.

Ace cameraman William H. Clothier was another Wayne stand-by, responsible for the stunning photography in such films as *The High and the Mighty*, *The Alamo* and many others.

Prestigious as his company was, John Wayne's first picture under the Wayne-Fellows banner was a resounding bomb. *Big Jim McLain* was a spy thriller in which an Un-American Activities investigator (guess who?) breaks up an espionage ring in postwar Hawaii.

At the time, Duke had just taken up the cudgels for the Motion Picture Alliance for the Preservation of American Ideals, the organization sworn to prevent Communist infiltration in the movie industry. To say that his timing was bad would be putting it mildly. Pro-Communist or not, reviewers branded the film as blatant anti-Red propaganda, and would have none of it.

To make ends meet, Duke went to work in outside films, but Wayne-Fellows hung on and at last came into its own in 1954 with a fine vintage Wayne Western, *Hondo*. On top of that, the company scored another success in 1954 with *The High and the Mighty*, with

Duke's portrayal of the dependable co-pilot of the doomed airliner one of his best.

Later, the name of the company was changed to Batjac Productions, a name Duke took from the story of *Wake of the Red Witch*, in which Batjac was the name of the powerful maritime company which controlled the fates of the ship *Red Witch*, the beleaguered, embittered Captain Ralls, and of the girl the captain (played by Duke) loved—played by Gail Russell.

Whatever significance the name may have had, Batjac got off to a bad start. In spite of the presence of Lauren Bacall, *Blood Alley* was a slow, disappointing sea saga. This was followed by a disaster in the desert—*Legend of the Lost*, co-starring Sophia Loren and Rosanno Brazzi. None of the trio's undoubted talents could dig this one out of the sand.

After a total of ten films, Duke and Robert Fellows had dissolved their partnership, and Duke kept what was left of Batjac.

Things weren't as tough as they appeared. Duke had a fabulous contract going on the side with 20th Century-Fox, who had signed him for three pictures over three years, for two million dollars! Tax-wise, they gave him another break—it would be paid at the rate of $200,000 a year for ten years.

That would be enough for anybody to retire on for life, when they're forty-nine. For Duke, it wasn't that simple, by a long shot. Not only did he have two families to support and high taxes to pay, but there were a thousand other expenses and hordes of people dependent on him for their livelihood. No, he couldn't quit. Besides, he had things to do, and dreams to dream . . .

he wouldn't have quit, no matter what. He had one dream he wanted to fulfill, at least.

His biggest and most expensive dream was *The Alamo*.

Chapter 16

REMEMBER THE ALAMO!

"I've got everything I own in it. But I'm not worried in the least bit. This is a damned good picture. It's real American history, the kind of movie we need today more than ever. It'll make money for years to come."

There's something about making a move that tantalizes every producer. The possibilities of the medium itself are so tremendous that anyone with money to spend, and a movie to make, is sorely tempted to pour it all into the pot to stir up the biggest, greatest picture ever seen.

Even more tantalizing is the knowledge that some of these films, produced at enormous cost, have paid back the investment many times over. Some—but not all.

D. W. Griffith's *Birth of a Nation*, the first big war film, took the country by storm. Its battle scenes were so well done that they are still models today. In contrast, Griffith's *Intolerance*, a rather vague morality play featuring monumental re-creations of decadent ancient times and thousands of extras, was a total failure.

Ben Hur, *The Ten Commandments*, *Gone With the Wind* were three more superspectacles that made it big at the box office. On the other side of the ledger, you could list such super-dogs as *War and Peace* and *Cleopatra* (23 million dollars, plus Liz and Burton, didn't keep her barge from sinking).

When John Wayne decided that, come hell or high water, he was going to make *The Alamo* the biggest, greatest picture ever, he wasn't thinking of monetary returns. This was the fulfillment of his dream to recreate for the American people one of the finest chapters in their history—the thirteen days from February 23 to March 6, 1836, when a small band of 180 Americans under the leadership of Colonels William B. Travis, James Bowie and Davy Crockett held off 4,000 Mexicans under Santa Anna and perished in a delaying tactic that gave General Sam Houston time to mass his forces and drive out the enemy.

It was a story dear to John Wayne's heart, embodying all the values he believed in—do-or-die patriotism, the universal fight for freedom, the epic courage of the heroes of the Old West. Everything.

If he wasn't interested in making money, he had to be

interested in raising it to make the picture. He'd formed
an arrangement with United Artists for release and
distribution of his Batjac productions, and they agreed
to advance him part of the total cost, which he estimated
at $6 to $8 million. This would have been enough to
finance General Sam Houston's entire campaign, but it
was only the beginning.

In search of authenticity, a site was chosen near
Brackettville, a town numbering less than 2,000 just
east of the Rio Grande and the Mexican border, 100
miles west of San Antonio.

The authenticity was fine, but any old Army man
could have told them that the logistics left a lot to be
desired. Logistics, as the original defenders of the
Alamo knew only too well, is the military problem of
getting enough of the right thing to the right place at the
right time.

At a cost of $1,500,000, replicas of the Alamo mis-
sion and San Antonio were reconstructed. So far, so
good. But then, the casting crew had to comb every
town for miles around to recruit the 4,000 extras to
serve as Santa Anna's hordes.

A lot of them had to have horses, so that meant
getting 1,500 of them, with arrangements for their care
and feeding. In addition, head wrangler Bill Jones had
to travel 35,000 miles to buy stock, including prized
Texas longhorns, at whatever the going price was.

The worst was yet to come. Once assembled, the cast
had to be fed, and without a miracle from on high,
Brackettville's grocery stores couldn't do it. Huge
walk-in refrigerator-freezers had to be shipped to the
site, together with huge quantities of food—40,000
steaks, 14,000 pounds of roast beef, 14,000 pounds of

ham, 4,800 pounds of sausage and bacon. Then, a whole crew had to be recruited to prepare the stuff. The total cost, at the end of the 81 days' shooting, was $250,000. It was enough to make the original defenders of the Alamo turn over in their graves.

It was also enough to make John Wayne's ulcer kick up, but he just stopped drinking Scotch. The cost of the food was almost enough to make him stop eating, too. But he pressed grimly onward. United Artists came through with more cash—but not much. The costs were now soaring far beyond the first estimates.

Right there, the fall of *The Alamo* began, because Duke, who was the director and producer as well as playing the role of Davy Crockett, had to go scrounging for money. He pleaded, he begged, he borrowed, and he wound up mortgaging everything he owned—the oil wells, the real estate, the uranium mines, even the shrimp boats—to pay the costs, which by the end of production had reached 12 million dollars.

On top of that, two scandals, in which he wasn't directly involved, hit the headlines and gave the papers a field day.

The first occurred when Duke and Frank Sinatra went to a costume party at the Moulin Rouge in Hollywood for the benefit of SHARE, an organization that helps retarded children. The theme was Western, and Duke came in his usual cowboy duds. Frank killed 'em as an Indian squaw. Both got up and sang for the cause, Duke groping his way through ''Red River Valley'' and Frank going into his usual expert rendition of ''The Lady Is a Tramp.'' They were both a hit and the evening was a big success.

Unfortunately, they ran into each other outside.

Shortly before, Sinatra had hired Albert Maltz, a writer who had been jailed for refusing to tell whether or not he was a Communist, to write a screenplay for *The Execution of Private Slovic*. Maltz had been blacklisted in Hollywood, and Sinatra was pressured into letting him go, and he still blamed John Wayne for a good bit of that pressure.

When they met in the parking lot, Duke said genially, "Hi, Frank."

Sinatra stiffened. "You don't seem to agree with me," he said.

"Let's discuss this some other time," Duke said. With that, Frankie took a swipe at him, which was something like a pebble hitting Mount Rushmore.

Friends intervened, and Duke strode off to his car. Frankie, still fuming, somehow strode into the path of a lot attendant, Clarence English, who jammed on the brakes of the Thunderbird he was driving just in time.

Frank tried to pull him out of the car, ripping his shirt. Another attendant, Edward Moran, came to English's defense. "Look, Frank," he said, "he didn't mean it. He wasn't trying to run you down—why should he?"

Frank swore and pushed Moran away. Moran came back and hit him with a right cross.

Before anybody could throw another punch, a huge man, over six feet and weighing about 220 pounds, grabbed Moran, hurled him against a car and beat him. Two other attendants pulled the man off Moran, who had to be taken to Hollywood Receiving Hospital for treatment.

Moran signed an assault complaint against Sinatra and his "bodyguard," "John Doe." Police stated that

DUKE

Sinatra had been drinking. Frankie said he didn't have any bodyguards, drunk or sober, and he'd pay $10,000 to anybody who could prove it.

It was all pretty weird, but one thing was clear. If Sinatra hadn't tangled with John Wayne and got himself all upset, it probably wouldn't have happened.

At least, on the bright side, the cause of SHARE got an awful lot of free publicity.

The next publicity that hit John Wayne during the making of *The Alamo* didn't have a bright side.

Along with other starlets who were hired in Hollywood for the big-budget picture was a pretty girl named La Jean Ethridge. She was twenty-seven, hadn't been doing too well and was glad to get the work, even though it meant living in cramped quarters with other extras. La Jean's quarters turned out to be a bunkhouse in nearby Spofford, shared by five men. This didn't turn out to be such a big problem. Apparently, La Jean settled on one of them, thirty-two-year-old Chester Harvey Smith, who became her lover.

La Jean had a bit part in the movie, but she was so good that she caught Duke's eye and he elevated her to a featured role and her salary from $75 to $350 a week.

Gleefully, she went back to the bunkhouse and started packing to move to better diggings in Brackettville. In walked Chester.

"Where you going?" he demanded. After all, if you live with a girl for four weeks, you've got a right to know, haven't you?

La Jean told him and kept on packing. There was a big argument. Then Chester picked up a bowie knife and plunged it into La Jean's chest.

The police found her dead, in a pool of her own blood, with Chester mumbling as they led him away to be charged with murder, "I couldn't live without her. . . ."

It might have gone by as a routine crime-of-passion murder if Fred Semaan, the San Antonio attorney defending Chester, hadn't decided to subpoena John Wayne as a witness at the hearing. Like an instant plague, the press descended on quiet little Brackettville in droves.

Justice of the Peace Albert Postel tried his best to keep the peace by ordering a closed hearing. It made the press less peaceful. John Wayne's attorneys and the State's Attorney wanted everything out in the open, but Justice Postel kept his peace.

Other men who had known La Jean and Chester marched in and out. Some stayed quite a long time. Then John Wayne marched in and out, in a short time. To inquiring reporters, he could only say, "I'm bound by the court's order not to reveal my testimony."

Completely thwarted, the press departed. It wasn't until much later that the facts came out. There was no jury trial because Chester pleaded guilty and was sentenced to twenty years. He was paroled in seven-and-a-half.

As for John Wayne, his only involvement was that Chester's lawyer felt he had been pushing to get the case over with so it wouldn't interfere with his expensive movie. The lawyer thought that would be to his client's detriment, so he sent Wayne a subpoena. Wayne threatened not to show up. The lawyer threatened to have him thrown in jail. Wayne showed up.

When he walked in to testify, steaming, Chester's lawyer made him even hotter by deliberately calling him "John Payne."

Finally, Duke shouted, "I'm not Payne—I'm Wayne!"

Actually, in view of Chester's plea, Duke's testimony was quite irrelevant, but the attorney couldn't resist deflating him a bit, this big producer who was so used to giving the orders.

Afterward, outside the courtroom, Duke told him, "Well, I guess I asked for that." He grinned, the two shook hands and became good friends!

Meanwhile, back at the location, retired Marine Corps Sergeant Jack Pennick, a hero of the 6th Marines in the World War I battle of Belleau Wood, was drilling the 4,000 extras who comprised Santa Anna's army in charging with real bayonets fixed to genuine flintlock rifles. Fifty gunsmiths were needed to keep the rifles in condition, and every time a volley was fired it cost $1,500.

It was another instance of the painstaking care with which John Wayne sought to make *The Alamo* historically accurate, down to the last detail.

A lot of time and effort had gone into the film before it went into production. James Grant, who wrote the screenplay, had put in nine years of research into the lives of the Alamo heroes. Al Ybarra, Batjac's art director, had studied for eight years to build his wonderfully realistic sets.

The cast had been chosen with care. Laurence Harvey was given the role of Colonel Travis, commander of the little army. Harvey's sophistication was well suited to the part of Travis, who was an aristocrat and a charmer with the ladies.

Richard Widmark was a perfect choice for Colonel James Bowie, a hard-bitten cynic who commanded a tough group of volunteers.

Duke himself was just right as the older Davy Crockett, then an ex-Congressman from Tennessee, who had traveled 1,500 miles on horseback to fight, and die, at the Alamo.

As usual, the Wayne family was much in evidence. Michael was his dad's right-hand man as assistant producer, Patrick had a strong role as Captain James Butler Bonham, and Aissa, then four, made her movie debut as a little girl who flees the fort on the back of a mule.

As producer-director, John Wayne might have been better off if he hadn't chosen such a monumental film as his first effort. Nevertheless, in spite of all the hangups and expense, he did get the film finished in the allotted 81 days—and that was no small feat in itself.

But the smoke had hardly cleared from the flintlock blasts at Brackettville before war clouds were gathering in Hollywood for a different kind of fight over *The Alamo*.

This time, it was a war of words, and the ammunition was advertising.

The first shots were fired by John Wayne, who took out a two-page spread in *Life* which set him back $152,000. The ad, prepared by Wayne's publicist, Russell Birdwell, proclaimed "There were no ghost writers at the Alamo . . ." and the text, signed by John Wayne, was not so much a plug for the picture as a statement of his political beliefs.

The presidential campaign was going strong, with John F. Kennedy making his bid to overthrow the Republican administration, represented by Richard M. Nixon. In view of that, Wayne was questioned about the wisdom of taking out an ad to vent his own opinions.

"Because I'm an actor I don't think I should be robbed of the right to speak," Wayne retorted. "By taking out this ad I hoped I might prompt more motion picture companies into taking out institutional ads with a more patriotic attitude in the text."

He went on to say that he felt that politics were "smothering the individual" and he'd like to find a man, "Republican or Democrat or whatever, who really says what he thinks." He pointed out that the heroes of the Alamo were young men who thought and cared deeply about their country, and there ought to be more of that, especially with an election coming up.

Nothing wrong with that—except that some critics thought that taking out a $152,000 ad to state your political beliefs, no matter what they were, smacked of megalomania.

One of those who blasted Duke was writer James Heneghan, who had formerly been employed by him. They'd had a disagreement about money due Heneghan for his help in financing *The Alamo*, and Heneghan wound up suing Duke, claiming he was promised $100,000 and only got $9,000. The suit was settled out of court and the terms were not revealed. Regardless of how he came out of it, Heneghan's anti-Wayne feelings apparently still rankled.

"Wayne likes to believe that he is relentlessly honorable and that his word is his bond,'' Heneghan wrote. "This is not true, anymore than it is true that any man is entirely honorable. He would like to be in life a John Wayne character in a movie, but he has never quite made it.''

As time for the voting for the Academy Awards approached, *The Alamo* became the focus of one of the most fantastic, and unintentionally funny, ad campaigns that ever hit the Hollywood trade papers.

When two local movie critics took Birdwell to task for what they considered a too-expensive publicity and ad campaign for the picture, he took out four full pages in each of the Hollywood trades to criticize *them*. Birdwell was particularly irked by film critic Dick Williams, who had deplored the effect of the ads. "Oscar voters are being appealed to on a patriotic basis,'' Williams wrote. "The impression left is that one's proud sense of Americanism may be suspected if one does not vote for *The Alamo*. This is grossly unfair. Obviously, one can be the most ardent of patriots and still think *The Alamo* is a mediocre movie.''

On top of that, Chill Wills, who played the Beekeeper in *The Alamo*, got into the act. He had been nominated for Best Supporting Actor and, as is customary in Hollywood, his publicity man took out ads in the Hollywood trades to hypo his chances.

Chill Wills later claimed that it was all the publicity man's doing, but whoever was responsible went all out, even sending circulars to members of the Academy! In these, and in his trade ads, Wills appealed to his "cousins" to vote for him.

This prompted Groucho Marx to take out a trade ad

of his own. "Dear Mr. Chill Wills," it read. "I'm delighted to be your cousin, but I voted for Sal Mineo. Sincerely, Groucho Marx."

At the Screen Writers' Guild dinner, Mort Sahl suggested that Groucho should be awarded a special Oscar for "the best ad for nomination for an Academy Award."

Wills' ad campaign reached its lowest point in an ad that showed a poignant scene of the beleaguered defenders of the Alamo. The caption read, "We of the cast of *The Alamo* are praying harder than the real Texans prayed for their lives in the Alamo, for Chill Wills to win the Oscar. . . ."

John Wayne was so incensed that he took out *another* full page ad, blasting Chill for his "bad taste." He also made a statement: "No one in the Batjac organization or the Russell Birdwell office has been a party to Mr. Wills' trade-paper advertising. I refrain from using stronger language because I am sure his intentions were not so bad as his taste."

Chill Wills protested that he didn't know a thing about the infamous ad, that it was all his publicity man's doing.

Columnist Joe Hyams got in the last word. "The battle between Messrs. Wayne and Wills seems to be a high point in the Hollywood battle raging around *The Alamo*, which threatens to make the original scrap look like a skirmish. There are those in Hollywood, including this writer, who think that for Mr. Wayne to impugn Mr. Wills' taste is tantamount to Jayne Mansfield criticizing Sabrina for too much exposure."

Most upset by the whole thing were members of the

Academy, who threatened to take measures to prevent *any* advertising in connection with the nominations in the future, if this sort of thing continued.

Whether it had anything to do with it or not, it turned out that *The Alamo*, though it received nine nominations, didn't win a single Oscar.

It's also possible that the national ad campaign, especially the *Life* ad, turned off some people who didn't like patriotic propaganda with their movies.

At any rate, the picture John Wayne hoped would be another *Gone With the Wind* didn't do well, critically or at the box office. The expected flood of money to pay back that $12 million the picture cost didn't happen. It wasn't until years later, when Wayne sold a large piece of his interest in the film to United Artists, that he managed to break even. Only eleven years after its release, in September 1971, *The Alamo* was sold to TV.

If the picture had its faults, it also had many virtues and deserved a better reception. In the battle scenes, and the hand-to-hand fighting, John Wayne displayed real mastery as a director. In particular, the scenes where the 4,000 of Santa Anna's men storm *The Alamo* are breathtaking.

Some felt the picture suffered because Harvey had the dominant role, and Wayne, the big box-office draw, played a minor part in comparison. More likely, it suffered because by acting, directing and producing, Wayne was trying to do too much. What was most needed, however, was a firm hand in the cutting room. The picture was too long, it rambled, and the characters were given to uttering boring little patriotic pronouncements that only had the effect of slowing down the genuinely impressive patriotic action.

If he hadn't had his contract with 20th Century-Fox to fall back on, John Wayne would have been bankrupt. He escaped his own *Alamo*, but it would take him years to rebuild his fortune.

Chapter 17

THE MAN ON HORSEBACK—THEME AND VARIATIONS

"A man on horseback has always been the top hero. Look at the monuments—they're always a man on horseback!"

———————◆◆◆———————

If *The Alamo* was a dream that developed nightmarish overtones, a happier dream came true for the Duke the night he received his Oscar for the role of Rooster Cogburn in *True Grit*. With Oscar in hand, though, he had to face the question raised by every triumph—"Where do I go from here?"

Ever since *The Long Voyage Home* in 1940, the Duke has experimented with non-Western roles. Early in the seventies, he received the script of *Dirty Harry*, but turned down the part after thinking it over carefully. He was attracted to the idea of working with Don Siegal, who was going to direct the picture, but the Duke knew that ruthless Harry was not a John Wayne character. (The movie became, of course, one of Clint Eastwood's biggest hits.) Reading that script did get the Duke interested in playing a policeman, and he was soon sent a script in which he would play a Seattle cop fighting corruption within the force. Now *that's* a John Wayne character—and *McQ* was his first cop role.

McQ broke one other precedent. Of the many, many leading ladies who have vied for the Duke's onscreen favors, it remained for Colleen Dewhurst, in 1973, to lure him into bed.

The Duke found that he enjoyed the role of law enforcer, and *Brannigan* (1975) starred him as a Chicago detective on special assignment to Scotland Yard.

But during the seventies, the Duke scored his biggest successes while playing the Man on Horseback. In *Rooster Cogburn* (1975), he swung back into the saddle and back into his Oscar-winning character. Like most sequels, this lacked the full power of the original story, but *Rooster Cogburn* teamed the Duke with Katherine Hepburn and provided moviegoers with a rare glimpse of two very different acting styles at work, and of two stars—equally feisty, durable and inimitable—striking sparks out of the contrast between their personalities.

Critics say that the Duke's most important movies

since *True Grit* are *The Cowboys* (1972) and *The Shootist* (1976). Both, while employing the John Wayne image—the Man on Horseback—also added new elements. The Duke isn't afraid to try new things—he knows he must vary his classic formula so it doesn't get stale.

The Cowboys (1972) departed from the formula when the Duke was killed off in mid-picture. Now, John Wayne has been shot in many a Western, and he has died eight times on screen. But until *The Cowboys*, those onscreen deaths had occurred in non-Westerns such as his war movies. In his Westerns, the Duke could be injured, but not killed. That would mean that John Wayne had *lost* his fight with the bad guys—and that's unthinkable!

The scriptwriter for *The Cowboys* got around the unthinkable. He worked out a plot in which even though the Duke's character is murdered, he still wins out over the bad guy in the end. The group of young boys the Duke has organized to help him carry out his cattle drive succeed in his plan after his death—even though the villain, played by Bruce Dern, does everything he can to stop them all. The bad guy does murder John Wayne, but he can't stop the cattle drive—or the Duke's young recruits. The formula of all Westerns, that good will triumph over evil, is finally upheld, even though the John Wayne character doesn't live to see his victory.

The Shootist was released in 1976 and is John Wayne's most recent movie. Because of its plot, some wonder if he designed it to be his last. *The Shootist* opens with cuts from some of the Duke's finest Westerns. The hero, an aging gunslinger (the early Old West term was "shootist"), has had a glorious past. But he has learned that cancer will soon claim his life. Hero to the end, John Bernard Books decides to cheat destiny—and arranges to die in action. Because of the clips from early John Wayne westerns and because of Books's death at the end of the movie, *The Shootist* has been considered a "farewell" movie. It did reverse the John Wayne pattern: a resounding critical success, it did disappointing business at the boxoffice. Maybe its "farewell" flavor explains why the millions of John Wayne fans never flocked to see it. Who wants to accept the last word on the Duke?

Though he hasn't appeared in a move since *The Shootist*, the Duke has stepped up other activities in recent years. In 1974, he appeared in the opening segment of *Maude*, Norman Lear's frequently controversial situation comedy. And he has hosted several television specials on American and movie history. The highpoint in the Duke's recent television appearances probably occurred during a salute devoted to him which aired on November 28, 1976. After a number of speeches by celebrities, alternately comic and touching, Maureen O'Hara appeared onstage, and sang "I've Grown Accustomed to His Face" as the screen showed clips taken from the many movie scenes she and the Duke have played together.

And it's not only television that has been claiming the Duke's attention. In 1973, he became a recording star when he narrated "America—Why I Love Her." John Mitchum, the brother of Duke's friend Bob, wrote this tribute to American values, and the record scored a solid hit. Three years later, a book with the same title appeared, with Duke as co-author.

The political dimension of the book and the record made them both quite controversial. But even more troubling—to everyone but the Duke—was a recent decision to do TV commercials. His advisers and friends were worried—once more—about tarnishing "The Image." Why, why would he do such a thing?

"Hell—for the money, acourse!"

As long as the Duke believes in a product, he sees no threat to his integrity in helping to sell it. Especially when advertisers, aware of John Wayne's sincerity and believability, will pay top dollar to have his endorsement.

If Duke isn't a wealthy man by Hollywood standards, it hasn't kept him from becoming active in charity, especially in those devoted to children. He has given both time and money to a center for battered children in Beaumont, California, and a Pavilion for cancer treatment at the Variety Children's Hospital in Miami, Florida, will be named after him.

In September of 1978, a John Wayne dinner raised $423,600 towards the purchase of a 577 acre Boy Scout Camp, to be called the "John Wayne Outpost Camp."

Even outside his movie roles, the Duke retains the epic quality of the Man on Horseback. Or as Eagle Scout Bruce Faux said during that John Wayne dinner, "Sure, he plays characters bigger than life. But he has to. He is bigger than life."

Chapter 18

THE FIGHT THAT NEVER ENDS

"Sure, I wave the American flag. Can you think of a better flag to wave? Sure, I love my country with all her faults. I'm not ashamed of it and never have been. Never will be!"

———————◆◈◆———————

Back in 1948, a worried movie executive telephoned John Wayne.

"Duke, I've got to warn you," he said. "You're going to be in big trouble if you don't get out of that MPA. You just don't realize how much this kind of thing can hurt your career. Your box-office showing will fall. You'll hit the skids!"

"Thanks for the warning," Duke said, "but one thing I hate is this attitude that an actor's going to be ruined if he becomes involved in anything political. Hell, a butcher or a baker can say what he thinks, but not an actor. It's not fair!"

"You've got to be sensible about this, Duke," the man said, patiently. "I don't think I have to tell you how many enemies you're making in Hollywood. It'll give you a bad name with the producers. And when they don't want to hire you, you're finished!"

"Damn it, those people *are* my enemies!" Duke exploded. "What'd you expect me to do, cuddle up to the Communists?" Then he cooled off a bit. "I know you mean well, and I appreciate that. But I'm doing something I *have* to do."

The man sighed. "Okay, Duke, have it your way. Good luck."

They were talking about the newly formed Motion Picture Alliance for the Preservation of American Ideals, an organization dedicated to fighting the inroads of communism in the film capital. Among its members were some of Hollywood's biggest names—MGM production head James McGuinness, ace directors John Ford, Leo McCarey and Sam Wood, Adolphe Menjou, top writers Boreen Chase and Morrie Ryskind, Ward Bond, Roy Brewer of the AFL and, of course, John Wayne.

Although they were to be accused of it many times, these men weren't witch-hunters. There is no question that, in 1948, the movie industry had been heavily infiltrated by communism. Only a small minority were actually whole-souled, card-carrying party members. To the vast majority, communism had become "fashionable.'' The creative people—the players, the artists and writers—who are the lifeblood of Hollywood, fell for it under the guise of liberal idealism. Because creative people are seldom politically astute but tend to become starry-eyed over vague ideas of ''progress'' and ''brotherhood,'' they were an easy prey.

Many of the movie executives, if not actual sympathizers themselves, tended to look the other way. So long as these talented people made money for them and didn't make much noise in public, they didn't care.

Their indifference boomeranged when the Un-American Activities Committee turned its investigations to Hollywood. When the smoke cleared, ten writers went to jail for refusing to tell whether or not they were Communists.

Thereafter known as The Unholy Ten, they included men who had contributed brilliant work to Hollywood films. Nevertheless, in a red-faced move to avert public disfavor, the ten were blacklisted, unable to get work from movie moguls long after they had served their terms and paid the fines inflicted on them.

This had the effect of bringing the whole Communist thing into the light, and forcing everybody in the motion picture industry, from top to bottom, to take a stand. For years afterward, the whole business was split between those who cast their lot with the Left or with the Right. Though it may be less acrimonious today, that sharp division still exists.

At the time Duke and his friends formed the MPA, feelings ran high. On both sides, retaliations (which had nothing whatever to do with making good pictures) were rampant.

It was the kind of fight you couldn't win with a horse

and a rifle, but John Wayne plunged into it in true John Wayne style. As he saw it, he was carrying the standard of Old Glory against the enemy, as he had in many a film.

This wasn't such a simple war. The Rightist members of the MPA did suffer badly, as the movie executive who called Duke had predicted.

But their sufferings were imposed by their own people, their Leftist co-workers in the movie industry—not the public.

Actors with such fine records as Adolphe Menjou and Ward Bond suddenly found doors closed to them. Menjou gracefully retired. Ward Bond turned to TV and came back strong in *Wagon Train*. The brilliant writers and directors suffered, too, from rejection.

As for John Wayne, it might be easy to say that he was too big, too powerful at the box office to have any of this hurt him. The stand he took, which cost his cohorts dearly, in his case looked like as empty a patriotic gesture as waving Old Glory on the way to the bank.

No, his stand didn't hurt him at the box office one bit, a fact that gave him enormous satisfaction. On the contrary, he kept right on climbing until, two years *after* he became active in the MPA, he was the top box-office draw in the country.

Where he was concerned, the attack was more subtle and even more devastating. From the time he joined the MPA and, along with the others, came out with a public statement of his stand against communism, every Leftwing writer, critic or columnist began to take pot shots at him.

Duke shrugged it off. He'd won his first big battle in

proving to the whole motion picture industry, once and for all, that an actor *can* be active politically without harming his appeal to the public one iota. Of all his achievements, this is the one of which he is most proud, because it went a long way toward liberating his fellow thespians so that they, too, could express their beliefs freely, no matter what their political persuasion.

He continued to take his opponents' fire with cheerful good humor. "You get to expect a certain kind of review," he says. "There's one guy on one magazine who's always pretty cute about me. Once he said I walked like a male Marilyn Monroe. But that didn't bother me. At least, it showed he was working hard to come up with something new."

The sniping didn't diminish. Every time a new John Wayne film came out, the "let's get him" boys were at him again, with their trusty typewriters. Naturally, they had a field day with *The Alamo*, because they could attack him from three sides—as actor, producer and director.

John Wayne knew enough about making movies to realize that bad reviews can affect them only to a point. In the long run, they have to stand on their own merits. Undoubtedly, his enemies did contribute to the downfall of *The Alamo*. They certainly didn't help.

But nothing—absolutely nothing—could make Wayne forsake his patriotic fervor.

By 1960, due largely to the beating he'd taken on *The Alamo*, he was broke.

Some time before, he'd confided to Hollywood writer Vernon Scott, "I've been acting almost thirty years, and I never came near to amassing a fortune. I'd like to take it easy for a while but I can't. I have to keep my head above water. By the time I pay off alimony, my business agent and manager and raise my kids, I'm lucky if I break even. I'm conservative. I don't throw big parties. I don't have expensive hobbies. I came along too late to make good investments before taxes. I keep working because I need the money. I need it bad.''

So he kept on grinding out movies, some of them very good—*The Commancheros, The Man Who Shot Liberty Valance, Hatari, McLintock, The Sons of Katie Elder*, to name a few.

He was working on another good one, *El Dorado*, with Bob Mitchum at Paramount in 1966, when he read Robin Moore's bestseller, *The Green Berets*.

For him, this exciting account of the U.S. Special Forces A-team in Vietnam was a natural. He'd hardly laid the book down before he was on the phone, trying to buy the rights for his company, regardless of the fact that Hollywood movie-makers had bypassed the Vietnam war as something too hot to handle.

Then it was the old story—trying to get backers. He knew that three of the studios had already dropped plans for pictures on Vietnam. So he went to two who hadn't, Columbia and Universal.

''Sorry, the cost would be too high,'' was their verdict. Wayne suspected they were just chickening out.

''I didn't think there was any doubt about this picture making money,'' he said. ''My record was pretty good.'' Apparently, it was going to take more than the potent Wayne name to get a studio to take on this hot potato.

Duke kept on trying. With him, it was a personal thing, an obligation he had to fulfill to the boys in

Vietnam who he'd recently visited on a USO tour. He'd promised them to let the American people know "what's going on over here."

He got his own taste of what was going on while visiting the 7th Marine Regiment near their base at Chu Lai. He was signing autographs when rifle shots cracked, hitting the dirt a few yards away. A squad went after the sniper but found only an abandoned bicycle.

"Those yella bastards always shoot from hiding, don't they?" Duke remarked, and went on signing autographs.

Finally, he was able to make a deal for the movie with Warner Brothers—Seven Arts, though he admitted it was a rough one. They were willing to invest $7 million, but as actor and director he had to accept a good bit less than he normally got.

The book was purchased for about $50,000, the screenplay got under way, and John Wayne went to work to arrange his chosen location—right in Vietnam. There was only one way to do that—go straight to the White House.

That building was then occupied by Lyndon B. Johnson, and in the 1964 campaign, Duke had done some strenuous campaigning for Barry Goldwater. However, LBJ had looked upon him approvingly when he was senior Senator from Texas, and Duke was down there glorifying his favorite state in *The Alamo*. The two had once met briefly at a Gridiron dinner, and Duke decided to write him a letter.

In a spirit of true Southern hospitality, LBJ overlooked the anti-Johnson speeches and, through his press secretary, Bill Moyers, expressed interest in the project. Moyers immediately contacted the Defense Department, who assigned a Green Beret, Major Jerold R. Dodds, as the first of several technical advisers on the film.

The first advice he got from the Defense Department was that Vietnam as a location was out. Not that they were disturbed by the Moscow paper, *Sovietshaya Kultura*'s attack on Wayne as an "extreme reactionary" who would find "real bullets" if he went to Vietnam. It was just that such a venture would be far too costly. (This was true, but it may have been just as true that the military took a dim view of being accused of catering to a bunch of Hollywood film-makers when there was a war going on.)

They did offer Duke a fine alternative—the facilities of Fort Benning, Georgia. They also gave him a lot of other things, at considerable expense, all of which was to come to light later on.

Even with all this assistance, Duke, again faced with the task of being both actor and director, began to fall behind schedule.

One day, a familiar Hollywood figure arrived in Fort Benning, dressed in a fur-collared coat and puffing a huge cigar. Duke took one look at famed director Mervyn LeRoy, who among his many hits had turned out such wartime winners as *Thirty Seconds Over Tokyo* and *Mr. Roberts*, and knew he hadn't come there just to look at the scenery. He'd been sent by the biggies at Warner Brothers, who were worried about Duke's sluggish pace.

LeRoy came right to the point. "I'm not here to interfere, Duke," he said affably, "but let's get this show the hell on the road."

Duke's glowering face broke into a grin like the sun coming through thunderclouds. "I know why you're here, Merv," he said. "It's those goddamn stockholders at the studio who think I'm draggin' my tail. I want you to know I've got nothin' against *you*."

The two shook hands. They had a few run-ins during the shooting, but they were minor skirmishes over camera angles and the like that didn't amount to much.

Even before the production began, John Wayne was the target of many attacks right at home, let alone Moscow. One fact his detractors overlooked was that he had chosen his cast without any consideration of their feelings about the war. "I don't give a damn," he said, "as long as they know their way around in movies and aren't afraid to get themselves messed up." He wound up with Aldo Ray, Jim Hutton, David Janssen, Raymond St. Jacques and Bruce Cabot in the leading roles—all of whom met his requirements but whose personal viewpoints differed widely.

As at *The Alamo*, Duke was in his glory in the action scenes, and at his best. Those who remembered that he'd had a lung cut out a few years before marveled at the way he took a beating that few of the younger men could endure—wading chest-deep in cold water to set up camera angles, running and climbing and shooting and falling in the mud—and loving every minute of it.

When everybody, including Director Wayne, had all they could take, he'd yell, "Cut!" and tell all the people how wonderful they were before he staggered off to a hot shower and a well-earned Scoth or two. After that, a big steak dinner.

What better way to end a perfect day? To him, it was just that—a day when, at last, he had a chance to pour all his talents into something he really believed in, a film that would fight the menace of communism throughout the world.

Maybe he'd made too many Westerns, but Duke had yet to learn that their simplified formula of the "good guys" versus the "bad buys" wasn't all that black-and-white in real life.

While the shooting was still going on, political snipers were piling up their ammunition. How come, they demanded, John Wayne got the use of a military post and personnel, with all the expense that involved? Who was paying for what?

The Army stoutly maintained that they supplied only material pertinent to the film that was not readily available, in the interests of accuracy. The "soldiers" used were real, all right, but they weren't working in the movie on the taxpayers' money, they were on their own leave time, and their work was paid for by the company.

To some curious politicians, the explanation wasn't good enough. What about the use of planes, and helicopters, and every kind of equipment that would have cost a fortune if the motion picture company was footing the bills? What about that bunch of Hawaiians up in Fort Devens, Massachusetts, who suddenly found themselves flown to Fort Benning on "administrative leave" for a most unexpected Army experience, acting as soldiers of the Vietnamese and Vietcong forces?

As a director who'd won his place at the top by turning out fine pictures in spite of tight budgets, Mervyn LeRoy had none of Duke's lofty illusions. As usual, he laid it on the line: "We wouldn't be getting all this stuff if somebody didn't want this picture made."

True to his word, LeRoy didn't take over the director's reins from Duke, but rather served the purpose he had been assigned of pulling the vast project together and seeing to it that it kept on schedule. Along with the others, he admired Duke's ability and his courage. "That crazy, wonderful son-of-a-bitch," he thought. "They don't make them like that in this business anymore."

Their combined efforts—plus those of Ray Kellog, the expert who handled the night scenes—were about to "bring the picture in," as they say in Hollywood, within the allotted $7 million, when nature played a disastrous trick on them. In the middle of November 1967, work was nearly completed when an early frost, most unusual for that time of year in Georgia, turned the lush green of their "jungle" to yellow and brown.

Nothing could be done but rush back to Hollywood, build an expensive "jungle" set and finish the picture there—at a cost of another million dollars.

When *The Green Berets* was released in July 1968, its reception was pretty much as John Wayne expected—blasts from the critics and success at the box office.

Even Wayne couldn't have predicted the virulence of the reviews that greeted the picture. One of the worst appeared in the usually restrained and distinguished *New York Times*. Critic Renata Adler assailed *The Green Berets* as "a film so unspeakable, so stupid, so rotten and false in every detail that it passes through being fun, through being funny, through being camp, through everything and becomes an invitation to grieve, not for our soldiers or for Vietnam (the film could not be more false or do a greater disservice to them) but for what has happened to the fantasy-making apparatus in this country. Simplicities of the right, simplicities of the left, but this one is beyond the possible. It is vile and insane. On top of that, it is dull. . . ."

A couple of weeks later, at least a portion of the press was eating its words. "*Green Berets*, Rapped as 'Vile, Insane' Film, is Boffo at Box Office" proclaimed *The Wall Street Journal*. "Despite what appears to be critical overkill, the film-going public is marching to the beat of a different drummer—to box offices across the country. . . ." the august *Journal* wrote.

This wasn't just an opinion. It was backed up by the solid figures duly recorded by that show biz Bible, *Variety*. The first two weeks' grosses had left no doubt that the picture was not only going to break even, but make money.

Whether they regretted being so harsh or not, *The New York Times* later came out with an article by their first-string movie critic, A. H. Weiler, who wrote, "John Wayne, who lost the first battle, has won the war as usual. *The Green Berets*, his controversial film about the unresolved seven-year American involvement in Vietnam, opened last June to a barrage of negative reviews, and is turning into one of the most successful movies released by Warner Brothers-Seven Arts in the last five years. It has earned, up to now, nearly $11 million."

Duke had his own explanation of what had happened. "I think those terrible reviews helped us a great deal. I've been in this business for forty years and any statements I've made have been pretty truthful, I think. When people read those reviews, I'm sure they

couldn't believe them. . . . *The Green Berets* simply
says that a lot of our brave guys are fighting and dying
for us out there. The ridiculously one-sided criticism of
the picture only made people more conscious of it and
they are proving that the reviews were not very effective.''

Why had the people ignored the reviews so completely? Michael Wayne came up with the best answer:
"Most critics reviewed the war and not the picture,
which is about people, not politics.''

It didn't do the picture any harm either when in 1969,
long after it had been released, a Democratic Represen-
tative from the New York borough of Queens, Benja-
min S. Rosenthal, made it the target of an attack,
charging that the Army "subsidized" the film by contributing men and equipment to the tune of about a
million dollars. He listed the time of 3,800 days put in
by Army personnel, the use of UH-1 combat helicopters, the use of rifles, machine guns, mortars, cranes
and trucks.

Wayne retorted that his company had been billed for
everything by the Pentagon, and, "Moreover, we spent
$171,000 on the base in building a camp they used after
we left. We in no way interfered with their business and
we never used one military person if he was on duty.''

The Army also came to his defense, stating that they
had charged for everything that was used.

Rosenthal, a brave man, proceeded to open fire not
only at John Wayne, but the whole Army. "The
glorified portrayal of the Vietnam war, which is the
heart of the film, raises serious questions about the
Defense Department's role in using tax funds for direct
propaganda purposes,'' he charged.

Wayne fired the last shot. He accused Rosenthal of using the whole controversy for publicity purposes, and defended *The Green Berets* as "one of the only films I know about that's expressly been making Americans appear heroes around the world."

The affair petered out with no casualties on either side. If anything, it boosted interest in the film still further. By this time, happy Warner Brothers-Seven Arts had raked in over $12 million—$4 million clear profit—with no end in sight.

John Wayne, who had sacrificed a great deal personally to make it, was happy too, with good reason. Single-handed, he had shown Hollywood moviemakers that shying away from controversial films wasn't just cowardly but was bad business.

In addition, he had the tremendous personal satisfaction of knowing that he had dealt a telling blow to his arch enemies, the Communists.

"As far as I am concerned, they are our enemy," he stated flatly. "The Communists are our enemy, not the Russian people. The Communist conspiracy is our enemy.

"I've seen what's going on over there. If you go into any depth on it—the war—it has to be almost that you're for it; if you're a decent person you can't let people be so oppressed, particularly when you've told them and the rest of the world that you'll stop it.

"The only way Vietnam could bring on a third world war is if Russia figures they can't win the world any other way. What the hell—they're gradually taking over weaker nations, pushing their leaders out windows, and finally crushing them after they win their own freedom, like in Hungary. That should have started a third world war. We'd been telling people, 'Stand up for your rights and we'll back you up.' We've been doing this for years, and it's about time we kept our word. . . ."

Chapter 19

THE RELUCTANT POLITICIAN

"I can't stand politics, but I get hooked into it more than anybody else. They say I'm a Right-winger, but I consider myself a liberal. I listen to everybody's point of view and reason it out in my mind, then try to do what I think is right."

———————————◆◆◆———————————

John Wayne's political beliefs are something like, "Which came first, the chicken or the egg?" It's hard to tell whether those stalwart "for God and Country" characters he's played on the screen for so long have fostered his staunchly conservative Republicanism, or whether his thinking has molded the characters.

Be that as it may, he has emerged as a larger-than-life Hollywood version of the extreme Right-winger.

One person who doesn't agree with that image is John Wayne. "They say I'm a Right-winger, but I consider myself a liberal," he claims. "I listen to everybody's point of view and reason it out in my mind, then try to do what I think is right."

You can bet that what he thinks is right is usually Right. For years, he has been an ardent and vocal supporter of conservative Republican candidates, locally and nationally.

His activity in politics dates back to the days of the great Hollywood upheaval over communism in the industry, when even those who had been quite indifferent were stirred into taking sides.

Duke had first become aware of the situation when he was working in *Back to Bataan*, which was directed by the talented Edward Dmytryk.

Dmytryk used to do a good bit of talking about "the masses" and "revolution" and this aroused Duke's curiosity. It didn't sound like the talk of a red-blooded American. It sounded more like communism to him.

Duke played dumb, and eventually was invited to "cell" meetings that proved to him he was right.

Later, Edward Dmytryk was one of those under fire in the Communist purge. Unlike others who refused to answer, he freely admitted that he had been a Communist in 1944 and 1945 but had since seen the error of his ways.

The firsthand knowledge of Communist activity in Hollywood spurred Duke into his first full scale political involvement—on behalf of Senator Joseph McCarthy. And off he went to the Republican National Convention in 1952 to support his man. When McCarthy didn't make a showing on the first ballot, Duke came home with an "I Like Ike" button and proceeded to beat the drums for Eisenhower.

This open gesture for McCarthy led many to label Wayne as an arch-conservative, a label that has stuck to him through the years. It isn't a true picture. When John Wayne says, "I consider myself a liberal," he has made a stand, on occasion, that tends to prove it.

During the existence of the Motion Picture Alliance for the Preservation of American Ideals, the group was split into two factions. One believed that anyone who had ever been a Communist wouldn't change, was not to be trusted, and therefore should be ostracized. The other group felt that there were many who had joined, perhaps out of mistaken youthful fervor, and later saw the error of their ways and should be accepted. It may come as a surprise to learn that Duke was definitely lined up with the latter group.

Once, publicly, he expressed his attitude when he came to the defense of Larry Parks. After making a brilliant debut in movies in *The Jolson Story*, Parks was caught up in the general investigation. Candidly, he said that it was true that he had been a Communist sympathizer, but that he had changed completely. Duke stood by Parks firmly, ignoring Hedda Hopper's sharp words in her column, chastising him and pointing out that "boys are dying in Korea."

Larry Parks' career was ruined, anyway. But he never forgot that the one person in Hollywood who had the guts to speak up on his behalf was John Wayne.

From the outset, Duke had no personal political ambitions. "I'm just not a political animal," he said, many times. What he did feel very strongly was a sense of conviction about political issues which, to him, was the same as action. The two went hand-in-hand.

So he continued to give all-out support to the Republican presidential tickets. On the local scene, he didn't always hew to the Grand Old Party line, but stumped for those he felt best qualified. One of these, of course, was Ronald Reagan. He worked for him tirelessly.

Once, his "vote for the best man" policy got him into trouble.

He had come to Miami Beach for the Republican National Convention and was scheduled to make one of the opening speeches. It turned out to be one of the few interesting highlights of the occasion.

When the band struck up "You Ought to Be in Pictures" and Duke strode onto the platform, the delegates who had been lulled to sleep by the previous seventeen speakers suddenly woke up. To a lot of them, seeing John Wayne in the flesh was more important than seeing all the candidates put together. And they were completely enchanted when he started to speak.

Wayne can't read a Teleprompter without glasses, and if he has a script, usually winds up talking off the cuff, anyway. Or, to be more precise, from the heart.

"Took me a long time to decide to stand up here," he drawled. "I'm about as political as a Bengal tiger."

He went on to tell the folks that "this party gives a damn" and that "a nation is more than a government, it's an attitude."

He told the crowd what he wanted for his little girl. "I want her to get a good start in life—get some values that some articulate few say are old-fashioned. I'm grateful for every day I spend in America. . . . I know this may sound corny, but the first thing I'm going to teach her is the Lord's Prayer . . . . and I don't care if she memorizes the Gettysburg Address, but I want her to understand it. . . ."

Thunderous applause greeted every statement, and as he strode offstage, again to the sound of "You Ought to Be in Pictures," it was clear that John Wayne was one person in the hall *everybody* supported.

Later, in the Fontainebleu bar, he voiced some sentiments that weren't likely to be so popular, at least with a lot of people who weren't attending the Republican Convention.

A drink in hand, he sounded off on some of his favorite subjects.

The "threat" of Left-wing liberals—"They're really radicals. Most of them in communications never finished college. I can see entering college as a Socialist, but if you leave college as a Socialist, you're out of your head."

The younger generation—"When I was a kid, we had pills, too. Ten of them cost a dollar, and if you took forty you could go on a trip. Only thing today is, you people make them important. You listen to these punks. We had hippies in my day. We used to call them bindlestiffs. They lived down by the tracks and never took a bath."

Law and order—"Ghettos? What about them? I never thought I'd live to see the day when I'd look at television and see cops standing there, not using God-given law when all that looting was going on."

He made it clear to one and all that he was a Nixon man, through and through.

So it was rather embarrassing when, sometime later,

three London reporters came out with a book called *An American Melodrama* about the 1968 presidential race. In it, the authors said, John Wayne was one of those who contributed to the campaign fund of George Wallace! In spite of his impassioned speech at the Republican Convention, they stated, one of the women in the department handling contributions in Montgomery had said that Duke had sent three weekly checks of $10,000 each, the last inscribed, "Sock it to 'em, George!"

Duke denied the story, but did admit that he had been approached by the Wallace force to "serve in the campaign."

"They suggested that I might even be the vice presidential nominee on the Wallace ticket. But I refused. Wallace, I suppose, had some sound ideas. But I've been a Nixon man for years. I supported Dick Nixon heavily. . . ."

Though there have been quite a few other offers of this nature, Duke doesn't talk about them unless pressed, and has consistently turned down all political offers.

Once, he was being strongly urged to run for Senator from California on the Republican ticket. With Ronald Reagan in the Governor's mansion and George Murphy already in a Senate seat, what could be better than an actor of John Wayne's stature?

Again, he refused. As he has often said, "I can't stand politics!"

What he can't stand is the wheeling and dealing, all the tricky maneuvering that goes with it. Like the heroes of all those John Wayne Westerns, he prefers to meet his enemies face-to-face and head-on.

Such an opportunity arrived in 1974, when the *Harvard Lampoon*, the humor magazine of Harvard College, sent the Duke a mock challenge to show his leathery face in ultra-liberal Cambridge. This mock confrontation appealed to his sense of humor—and his sense of dramatics. The Duke showed up on the appointed day in an armored personnel carrier loaned by the Army Reserves. (He would have liked a tank even better, but the authorities were worried about the weight of the tank rumbling over all those subway tunnels that run under Harvard Square.) Even in radical Cambridge, there were plenty of John Wayne fans to swell the turnout, and the day was accounted good fun by Right and Left alike.

Another potential confrontation was smoothed over by the Duke himself. He was scheduled to present an award to radical actress Jane Fonda at a Hollywood Women's Press Club dinner. Instead of the fireworks everyone expected, the Duke was both gracious and nostalgic. Referring to their seating arrangement, he quipped, "I'm surprised to see you at the right of me," and added warmly, "I've had the good fortune to know Jane's father for forty years, and I've enjoyed watching Jane and Peter develop into fine talents."

As the painful memory of Vietnam recedes, most of the liberals have declared a cease fire on the Duke. But he has also caught some flak from the conservatives in recent years. His support for the signing of the Panama Canal treaties surprised people who insist on thinking of him as a party-line arch conservative. When hate mail from the extreme right began to pour in, the Duke was philosophical. "I've been jolted by the extreme left. I guess a little from the extreme right won't hurt me too much.''

A few years ago, an admirer referred to the Duke as a super-patriot. The fan meant well, but he was promptly corrected, "I don't like the label of super-patriot. I think I feel just like about 160 million people do out of the 200 million people in the U.S.''

Many disagree with his ideas. But few would argue the point that his complete honesty about them and his sturdy independence put him a cut above the common herd of politicians.

In fact, it's part of the growing John Wayne legend.

Chapter 20

OPEN HEART SURGERY AT SEVENTY

"Even before I got hit with this I had a pretty high regard for the Man Upstairs. But He can't do it all alone . . . That's where man's basic nature steps in."

———————————◆·◆·————————————

The Duke's words are from an interview taped in 1974, in which he reminisced about his operation for lung cancer. But they apply just as well to his attitude toward the open heart surgery he faced in April, 1978. John Wayne is a God-fearing man, but he also believes the Lord helps those who help themselves. He's a fighter. And at Mass General hospital he fought his way back from radical surgery for the second time in his life.

It began as hospitalization for "bronchitis" at the Duke's local hospital in Newport Beach, California. But a month later, John Wayne had checked into prestigious Massachusetts General Hospital in Boston. The official word was that he was in for tests. Eager to protect their father from the curiosity of his public, the Duke's older sons tried to dispel rumors that he was seriously ill. They played his hospitalization down—or tried to. But it's hard to play down any matter concerning John Wayne. One of the Boston news stations broke the big story the day before Duke's surgery: John Wayne needed open heart surgery to replace a defective mitral valve.

The mitral valve, essential for proper heart function, is between the left atrium and the right ventricle of the heart—so the surgeons would be operating at the very center of the heart. It would be a very delicate procedure; and a hazardous one for a man of Duke's age.

While the hospital switchboard tried to cope with the hundreds of inquiries that poured in that night, John Wayne was consuming a steak dinner at a French restaurant in Boston. He had been allowed to check out for a quiet meal—before the surgery and the months of painful recuperation.

He pulled through beautifully. People were amazed at how quickly the Duke—at seventy!—recuperated. As he had fifteen years before, he downplayed the long hours of pain and frustration. Three weeks after open heart surgery, he was boarding a plane for California, grinning and saying, "I feel fine!" One of the reporters had to ask it: "Were you scared?"

"Ah, hell, sure!"

During those three weeks in Boston, 100,000 letters addressed to the Duke had poured into the hospital's mailroom. Less illustrious patients received the unexpected bounty of overflow flowers and candy originally sent to the Duke.

The surgery had its later complications. Hepatitis, a frequent complication of surgery when tranfusion has been necessary, forced him to rest at least seven hours a day. And late in 1978, he began to discuss with his doctors the possibility, when the hepatitis was gone, of finally doing something about the gall stones that had been bothering him for so long.

Chapter 21

FACING THE NIGHTMARE AGAIN

"I've licked the Big C before—and I'm going to beat this one, too."

————◆·◆·◆————

A few days before his scheduled elective surgery for gallstones, the Duke was interviewed by Barbara Walters. Speaking of the upcoming operation, he seemed to have a premonition. The surgery was expected to be routine. "But who knows what they'll find?" He then spoke with gratitude (and a humorous reference to Women's Lib) of the help of God through his many other illnesses: "The fact that He's let me stick around a little longer—or She's let me stick around a little longer—certainly goes great with me."

On Friday, January 12, 1979 the operation started early in one of the many surgical sites at U.C.L.A.'s huge Medical Center. It was scheduled to last for two hours. But the surgeons found a tiny spot on the stomach as they were removing the gall bladder. A small amount of stomach tissue was rushed to the pathology lab, and the word that came back wasn't good. The stomach tumor was malignant. The doctors continued the surgery, removing his stomach and stitching part of his intestines up into the space where his stomach had been.

For the second time, doctors exploring an unrelated health problem had discovered that John Wayne had cancer. For the second time, the Duke faces the most dreaded of all diseases.

It is going to be a hard fight to win. Lung cancer, which he licked in 1963, is among the deadliest forms of the disease. But one of the few considered even deadlier is gastric carcinoma, the one he's fighting now. Survival rates are low because the disease spreads very fast and is usually far advanced before there are symptoms. One specialist rates the Duke's chances for survival beyond one year as only one in ten. This is because a small amount of cancer was also found in the lymph nodes near his stomach, a sign that the disease had already spread beyond the stomach. When the lymph system has begun to spread the disease, further surgery is useless. Treatment with drugs and radiation can check the progress of the cancer, but they can seldom cure it. Considered statistically, the Duke's chance of making it through the critical five year period is very slim.

But the Duke is a lot more than a statistic. A spokesman for the U.C.L.A. Medical Center has praised his "strong physical condition and his positive attitude." Both should help the Duke in the long struggle ahead. He made a strong recovery from the surgery itself, waking up just one and a half hours after his nine hours under anesthesia, and startling personnel in the Intensive Care Unit, who hadn't expected to deal with an alert Duke for another several hours or even days.

His children have remained a solid front of support. All seven were at the hospital during the long operation, praying for their father and waiting for the news.

For the second time in twelve months, calls for the Duke are overwhelming a hospital switchboard. And even a staff accustomed to celebrity patients has been amazed at the outpouring of telegrams, calls, and cards. The U.C.L.A. Medical Center has seen its quota of movie stars as patients—but how many patients even among the stars, ever received a phone call from Queen Elizabeth II of England? Britain's leading John Wayne fan called during his operation—as did another queenly Elizabeth, Liz Taylor.

Duke will be 72 on May 26. He faces again the worry over recurrence which cancer patients say is the worst feature of the disease. He will have to modify his life-style. Protein is good for him, so he can still enjoy his steaks. But he will have to eat much smaller amounts of food, with greater frequency, because of the removal of his stomach.

He faces the special treatments and the fussing that everyone finds distasteful when ill, but which are especially irksome to an independent and active man like the Duke. No one can say if his will can prevail once again over the statistical probabilities. No one can say if he will lick the Big C a second time.

But, just as in his movies, he's got all of us on his side.

Chapter 22

"HELL, I'M NO LEGEND!"

"I figure legends are people who aren't around. Hell, I'm here and I'm planning to stay around awhile longer!"

———◆◆◆◆———

A lot of people would like to be called legends in their own time. John Wayne hates it.

"It makes me feel like some old fossil," he growls. "Hell, I'm not dead yet!"

Yet, he *is* a legend, last of the screen's hard-riding super-heroes, last of a long line that began with his boyhood idols William S. Hart and Tom Mix.

It's no accident that, no matter what other roles he may play, he never stays away from Westerns long. Of course, he's aware that this is good business because his public is most familiar with him in Stetson and spurs. But more than that, it's the role he's most familiar with because it's the one that identifies most strongly with his own character.

From the time when he was making two-reelers on Poverty Row, he's developed that character to give it a stature and dimensions the Western hero never had before.

What he's always been after is realism. "When I started making Westerns," he recalls, "the hero was a guy like Tom Mix, who always wore a white hat and rode a white horse. If he knocked a guy down, he'd stand there, patiently waiting for him to get up before he knocked him down again. And he never, never kissed the girl!"

Duke remembered what his dad had taught him— that rule about trying to stay out of fights, but if you do get in one, win it. "So, if a guy in a movie I was making hit me with a vase, I'd hit him with a chair," he says, "and that's the way we went on from there. I knocked the stuffing out of the goody-goody Boy Scout cowboy hero, and made him a believable guy."

Early in his career, Duke also developed a sharp eye for the way the action in a scene contributed to the development of his character.

Once, he was supposed to fire a shot across a bar where some extras were standing, drinking. He fired the fake shot, but the extras kept right on lounging at the bar. "Tell those guys to move their asses when I fire that shot!" Duke yelled at the director. "Who in hell would stand around like that if it was a real bullet?''

Always, if he had a beef with a director, it was about the way a scene should be played to make it better and more believable. He was professional about it, never petty or personal. To directors he admired, he gave unquestioning obedience. Those he did talk back to came to appreciate his criticisms, no matter how profane they might be at times, because they were usually valid and always made in an attempt to improve the picture.

Simply because he wanted to do the best possible job, no matter what he was being paid or how rugged the work was, he developed the quality of authority. Between the good-looking kid in *The Big Trail* and the mature, confident man in *Stagecoach* were eleven years of hard, tough seasoning that showed in his every move. From *Stagecoach* on, the legendary character of John Wayne was established.

It was a perfect blend of the personal and professional, with enough of the personal in it to be convincing. He was strong and fearless, he fought for the right and protected women and children, but always there was a touch of humor and human weakness.

That's his secret, the magic touch that makes the difference in that legendary character.

Often questioned about the violence in his films, he replies, ''I don't think that my pictures are violent. The characters are usually rather likeable. Fights with too much violence are dull. The violence in my pictures is lusty and a little bit humorous, because humor nullifies violence.''

He has, in addition, a sound sense of what is right for him.

When TV began to shake up the movie industry and many other actors were trying to adapt to the new medium, Duke turned his back on it.

Director Andrew McLaglen, son of Duke's good friend, Victor, buttonholed him one day. "I've got this great TV series coming up," he told Duke. "It's about a sheriff in a small Western town. He's got to be a big guy, somebody who dominates the whole show and ties it together. With you, I *know* it can be a big hit. Would you consider it?"

Duke shook his head and laughed. "Andy, I'm a movie actor. I've always worked in films where there's a lot of space, and I'm large as life. If people see me on that little screen, they'll think I shrank!"

Seeing Andy's crestfallen face, Duke felt bad and wanted to help. "I'll tell you what," he said. "There's a guy I've worked with in a couple of pictures I think would be just right for that part. He's big—about six-feet-four—and he's a hell of a good actor. Fellow named Jim Arness."

You guessed it—the show was *Gunsmoke* and James Arness was on his way to making his first million.

For a long time, Duke was a sharp critic of TV. He couldn't stand the fast pace that resulted too often in slipshod work. He was used to the slow, painstaking routine of movie-making. He could probably never have adjusted to making a series. But then, he didn't have to. While many other movie stars were turning to the TV treadmill to augment shaky movie incomes, he didn't need it, because he was one of the very few who could still get people to go to the movies.

He was seventy in 1977. Now pushing toward eighty, the legend still lives. And it will survive long after he does.

Chapter 23

THE END—AND THE BEGINNING

"No matter what, I'll always be part of the motion picture industry because I love it. And when I die, I don't want any big, solemn funeral. Just my family and friends, having a few belts and talking about the crazy old times we had together. . . ."

The Duke has lived a lot, and laughed a lot, and loved a lot—and all he wants is more of the same.

Some years ago, when things weren't going too well, he told writer Maurice Zolotow, "A man pays a high price for fame. He surrenders his private life, and often his happiness. I sometimes wonder if I wouldn't have been better off if I remained the easy going, never-care-for-tomorrow fellow I was when I started. Maybe it was getting married and having children that changed me, filled me with an urge to prosper and provide a better life and economic security for my family.''

At this point of his life, he has no regrets. He has accomplished more and enjoyed more than most of us. Above all, the threat of death that cancer brings has taught him that every moment of it was precious.

The rest of the time he has well organized. Mornings at the Newport Beach home where he moved to be close to his first love, the sea, are spent taking care of his business affairs with his secretary, who drives out from Los Angeles.

Afternoons are free time. If the children are in school, he may go over to the Country Club to play some chess or bridge with his cronies (he's expert at both).

Daughters Aissa and Marisa, and son John Ethan, are the joy of his life, along with all the Wayne children and grandchildren (who now number twenty). They're always in and out, but once a year, usually just after the holidays, they all gather at the Newport Beach home for a big celebration.

He loves taking his family out on his beautiful yacht, *The Wild Goose*. A converted minesweeper, it's a luxurious, glorious fulfillment of his early ambition to command a vessel on the rolling waves. And he couldn't be more delighted that young John Ethan loves the sea as much as he does. Together, the two have a wonderful time.

He will never quit working entirely, though—as he

did after his heart surgery—he may have to work on projects less time-consuming and strenuous than movies. A while back, he said, "I have much work to do and a lot of life to live. I intend to be around motion pictures for a while yet, and when I begin to creak at the hinges and take on the appearance of a tired water buffalo, I'll play character parts. Because I know my trade as well as the next man in Hollywood, I'll direct. But no matter what, I'll always be part of the motion picture industry, for it has been my life and I love it."

He's learned to enjoy TV, and appear on it occasionally, though he still laments the fact that movies are "chopped to pieces" to fit time schedules, and are interrupted by commercials. Nevertheless, he's had a giant screen installed at an angle in the bedroom, so that he can watch the late shows in comfort. "It's like eating peanuts," he complains. "You start watching, and the next thing you know, they're playing the 'Star Spangled Banner'!"

One of his happiest TV appearances occurred in the spring of 1973, when with many other celebrities— including President and Mrs. Nixon—he was able to pay public tribute to the man of whom he has often declared, "If it weren't for him, and his belief in me, I'd still be playing sheriffs in third-rate Westerns." Yes, the program honored America's greatest director, John Ford, then old and ill and no longer able to work. Few scenes on TV have been so moving as that of John Wayne and President Nixon, gently supporting him as he walked off the stage after accepting the honors heaped upon him.

On August 31, 1973, John Ford died of cancer at the age of seventy-six. Although Duke, among other close friends, knew he had been putting up a gallant fight for a long time, it was still a shock. "Only last week we had a drink together, and talked about old times," Duke said. "He was my heart—the best friend I ever had."

John Wayne knows the day will come when he, too, can no longer work in movies. But like his great friend, John Ford, he'll keep up his spirits.

"I like a lot of things going on," he's always said, and you can bet that's the way it's going to be.

Once, returning from the funeral of a departed friend, he said, "God, how I hate solemn funerals! When I die, take me into a room and burn me. Then, my family and friends should get together and have a few belts and talk about the crazy old times we had together."

Another time, he selected his own epitaph, from his Mexican friends: "*Feo, Fuerte y Formal*," which, in translation, means, "He was ugly, was strong and had dignity."

It couldn't be more fitting.

Those who know him—and the millions who know him only through his movies—hope that neither the funeral nor the epitaph wil have to be used for a long, long time.

But when the time comes, we hope somebody will remember. Because that's the way Duke wanted it.

And that's the way it should be.